NOBEL LECTURES

PEACE
1996 – 2000

Nobel Lectures
Including Presentation Speeches and Laureates' Biographies

Physics
Chemistry
Physiology or Medicine
Literature
Peace
Economic Sciences

NOBEL LECTURES
Including Presentation Speeches and Laureates' Biographies

PEACE
1996 – 2000

Editor

Irwin Abrams
Antioch University

NEW JERSEY · LONDON · SINGAPORE · BEIJING · SHANGHAI · HONG KONG · TAIPEI · CHENNAI

Published for the Nobel Foundation in 2005 by
World Scientific Publishing Co. Pte. Ltd.
5 Toh Tuck Link, Singapore 596224
USA office: 27 Warren Street, Suite 401-402, Hackensack, NJ 07601
UK office: 57 Shelton Street, Covent Garden, London WC2H 9HE

NOBEL LECTURES IN PEACE (1996–2000)

All rights reserved.

ISBN 981-238-001-9
ISBN 981-238-002-7 (pbk)

FOREWORD

The Oxford Dictionary of Contemporary World History tells us that the Nobel Peace Prize is "the world's most prestigious prize." Of course nobody can be certain in such matters, but if this is true, which we at the Norwegian Nobel Institute very much hope it is, then the Nobel Peace Prize is not only the most prestigious among the more than three hundred peace prizes we know about at the Nobel Institute, but it is also the most prestigious prize in any category.

I think there are four basic reasons for the prestige of the Nobel Peace Prize, whatever it might be. First, the Prize has been awarded since 1901 and it has therefore had ample time to establish its present position. Second, the Peace Prize belongs to a family of prizes, the Nobel family, and all those who belong to that family benefit from the relationship. On our own none of us would have had a position similar to what it is today. Third, on the whole the Norwegian Nobel Committee, which awards the Prize, has established a respectable historical record through the 102 years of the Nobel Peace Prize's existence. The Committee has certainly made mistakes; the omission of Mahatma Gandhi from the list of laureates probably being the most striking one. Yet, all human beings make mistakes, and it may be argued that the Nobel Committee has made rather fewer serious mistakes than one could have expected.

Finally, the Nobel Peace Prize has developed over the years. It took much too long for the Peace Prize to become a fully global prize, but in recent decades it certainly has become truly global with many laureates from all continents (with the exception of Australia). More women have been awarded the Prize. "Peace" has been redefined and human rights have become a most important category within that definition.

Alfred Nobel never gave any precise definition of what he meant by "peace." It has therefore been very much up to the Norwegian Nobel Committee to define the term. The Committee has always felt there were many different roads to peace; therefore there would be many different kinds of laureates. This open approach to "peace" can certainly be seen also in the period dealt with in the present volume.

In 1996 the Prize was awarded to Carlos Belo and José Ramos-Horta for their struggle against Indonesia's suppression of East Timor and for the area's right to self-determination. The Prize for 1996 was to provide a rare example of the power of the Prize at its very best. The award of 1996 was undoubtedly one among several factors behind East-Timor's independence in 2002.

In 1997 the Prize was awarded to the International Campaign to Ban Landmines and its coordinator Jody Williams. The Nobel Committee had given many awards to the struggle to reduce the importance of nuclear weapons in international relations; the award in 1997 was the clearest example so far of the Committee's willingness to applying the words "reduction of standing armies," one of the three criteria mentioned in Nobel's will, to the conventional field.

In 1998 John Hume and David Trimble were awarded the Nobel Peace Prize for their long struggles to bring peace to conflict-ridden Northern Ireland. Awards to statesmen for their work to end regional conflict was nothing new in the history of the Prize, but the Good Friday agreement of 1998 promised to bring an end to the bloodiest conflict in Western Europe after 1945.

In 1999 Médicins Sans Frontières was the recipient of the Prize. The very first Prize in 1901 had been given to Henry Dunant, the founder of the Red Cross, together with French pacifist Frédéric Passy. Later three prizes had been awarded to the Red Cross and two to the UN High Commissioner for Refugees, so the prize to MSF was another one in a long series of awards to humanitarian organizations and persons.

In 2000 the Nobel Peace Prize was awarded to South Korean President Kim Dae-jung for his long struggle for human rights in South Korea and for his "sunshine" policy of reconciliation with North Korea. No one symbolized South Korea's transformation into a democratic state better than Kim; his hopes for the sunshine policy were high and we shall all be following with great interest the results of that courageous policy.

In this volume published by World Scientific you can read the presentation speeches of the chairmen of the Norwegian Nobel Committee, Francis Sejersted until 1999 and Gunnar Berge for 2000, and the Nobel lectures of the laureates just mentioned. Thus the long series of volumes of Nobel speeches and lectures are brought up to 2000.

Geir Lundestad
Director, Norwegian Nobel Institute
April 29, 2003

INTRODUCTION

This volume presents the Nobel Peace Prize addresses and Nobel lectures for the years 1996–2000, following the six volumes previously published, which cover the years 1901–1995.[1] These publications were authorised by the Nobel Foundation in Stockholm and edited with the assistance of the Norwegian Nobel Institute in Oslo.[2]

The texts are based upon the Nobel Foundation's annual publication, *Les Prix Nobel*, which prints the speeches and other basic information concerning the Nobel prizes presented on the previous 10 December. On this day, the anniversary of Nobel's death, the prizes in every category are presented each year, the Peace Prize in Oslo and all the others in Stockholm.

Each entry in this volume is preceded by a brief explanatory introduction to the following texts, as printed in English translation or in the original English: the Norwegian Nobel Committee's announcement about the winner or winners, usually released to the press in October; the presentation address of the Committee Chairmen Francis Sejersted and Gunnar Berge, as translated into English from Norwegian; and, since 1992, words of acceptance and thanks by the laureates, which are included with their Nobel Lectures, marking a change from previous years, when the Nobel Lecture was scheduled to be presented on a later day. Also included in this volume are endnotes to the preceding documents, biographical and descriptive information about the laureates and a selected bibliography.

The official announcements of the Peace Prize, which appear here, were not printed in an authorised collection of Nobel documents before 1993. Since each announcement must be approved by the Norwegian Nobel Committee, it represents the only official document we have presenting the Committee's reasons for the choice. The speech of presentation may refer to the Committee's rationale as well, but it does not have to be approved by the Committee in advance, and it may represent the particular interpretation or emphasis which this Committee representative wishes to give.

The biographical or descriptive information about each prize winner has generally been reprinted from the volumes of *Les Prix Nobel*, where this is usually submitted by the laureates themselves. Where other sources have been used, this is indicated in editorial footnotes to the individual entries.

Finally, to make these volumes more useful, with each entry there is a brief list of reading suggestions, generally restricted to publications in English. For fuller information about the peace prize, its origins and how it has been administered by the Norwegian Nobel Committee, see the editor's authoritative reference work, which is referred to below.[3]

Since 1990 the award ceremonies have been held in the spacious auditorium of Oslo's city hall, where on the wall behind the rostrum the audience looks upon the exhilarating mural by Henrik Sørensen of "The People at Work and Celebrating". Eleven hundred persons can be accommodated here, far more than in the smaller hall of the university, which for many years had been the scene of the event. Old timers miss the sense of intimacy which the university auditorium afforded, but the authorities have fewer problems in meeting requests for tickets in this larger hall, while security can be much tighter, which was especially important at the 1994 Middle East award, and in the balconies encircling the seating area there are facilities for up to about three hundred photographers and reporters from the press.

The ceremony itself is simpler than in Stockholm, where the king himself presents the awards and more conventions as to dress and ritual are observed. In Oslo from the beginning in 1901, when Norway was still under the Swedish monarchy, it has been the chair or another member of the Committee who has made the presentation of the diploma and the gold medal to the prize winner or a representative. In the years 1995 to 1999, Committee Chairman Francis Sejersted gave the speech and made the presentation. In 2000, Committee Chairman Gunnar Berge took over this task.

Since Norway has been independent, the Norwegian king has usually attended these occasions, and King Harald and Queen Sonja were present every year (except 2000) for those covered in this volume. Special invitations are sent to the cultural and political leaders of the country and to members of the diplomatic corps, who fill the first rows of the hall. Between the presentations and the speeches, appropriate musical selections are played by an orchestral ensemble. The audience is equipped with headsets to listen to translations of the speech being delivered in whichever of the major languages may be preferred.

The ceremony is scheduled to last about ninety-five minutes, a little more when there is more than one laureate. Each laureate is given a limit of fifteen to twenty minutes for the acceptance and Nobel lecture, which is frequently exceeded, but the ceremony is usually concluded by the early afternoon, time to go back home or to the hotel and watch the telecast of the prize awards in Stockholm.

In the early evening there is usually a torch-light procession honouring the laureate, organised by an appropriate local group. This ends at the Grand Hotel, where the prize winners are lodged, and they come out on their balcony to receive the plaudits of the crowd. The next event is the formal banquet for the laureates at the Grand Hotel, which is hosted by the Norwegian Nobel Committee and followed by dancing. This is the high point of the Oslo winter social season.

In the five years from 1996 through 2000 there were eight prizes awarded, one in each of the two years, 1999 and 2000, and two in each of the other three. Human rights played a role in the 1996 award to the East Timorese leaders and also in the awards to Doctors Without Borders in 1999 and to Kim Dae-jung in 2000, but the award to the Doctors was also for humanitarianism, while the prize for Kim Dae-jung was also to further the peace process between North and South Korea. This peacemaking concept also figured in the 1998 prize to John Hume and David Trimble in Northern Ireland, as it had in earlier prizes, such as the 1994 prize to Arafat, Peres and Rabin, and the 1993 prize to Mandela and de Klerk. In sharing the prize of 1997 between the International Campaign to Ban Landmines and its international coordinator, Jody Williams, the Committee was recognizing Nobel's inclusion of disarmament in listing works for peace in his will. As in previous years, the Committee's decisions demonstrated the variety of the paths to peace.

According to the statutes of the Nobel Foundation, "It shall be incumbent on a prize-winner, whenever this is possible, to give a lecture on a subject relevant to the work for which the prize has been awarded." This injunction gives the laureate a great deal of latitude. The reader will find much variety in the ways the peace laureates have met the obligation of the lecture. They are very different personalities, they have followed different roads to peace, and they have chosen various ways to interpret the particular path taken.

It must not be forgotten that these statements were written first of all to be heard, not for a book. Nor were the prize winners chosen for their oratory. They were honoured for their deeds, not for their words. Yet there is eloquence here and high inspiration.

No one can miss the sense of commitment which moves most of these speakers nor the depth of their sincerity. Altogether the contributions collected here and in the previous volumes in this series represent an unrivaled documentation of the many ways in which some of the noblest spirits of our time have worked on the most crucial problem facing humanity today, the restraining of violence and the building of peace based upon human solidarity.

ENDNOTES

1. Irwin Abrams, editor. *Nobel Lectures. Peace 1971–1980* and *Nobel Lectures. Peace 1981–1990* (Singapore: World Scientific, 1997) and *Nobel Lectures. Peace 1991–1995* (Singapore: World Scientific, 1999).

   The lectures for the years from the first award of 1901 through 1970 are to be found in the exemplary volumes edited by Frederick S. Haberman, Nobel Lectures. Peace, 3 vols. (reprinted by World Scientific in 1999). These were also authorised by the Nobel Foundation. The format is similar to the present volumes, but there are extensive footnotes, a feature considered less needed for the present volumes, and biographical essays are written by Haberman, replacing the information submitted for *Les Prix Nobel* by the laureates themselves.

2. In particular, I wish to thank Anne C. Kjelling, Head Librarian of the Norwegian Nobel Institute.

3. Irwin Abrams, *The Nobel Peace Prize and the Laureates. An Illustrated Biographical History, 1901–2000*, centennial edition. (Nantucket, MA: Science History Publications/USA, 2001). See also Irwin Abrams, ed., *The Words of Peace. Selections from the Speeches of the Winners of the Nobel Peace Prize*, 3rd edition (New York: Newmarket Press, 2000). Another collection of Nobel peace lectures has been published by UNESCO in its Cultures of Peace series: *Peace! An Anthology by the Nobel Peace Prize Laureates*, edited by Marek Thee (Paris: UNESCO, 1995).

For other sources on the Peace Prize, see
<http://www.infography.com/content/194790504497.html>

CONTENTS

Foreword		v
Introduction		vii
1996	CARLOS FILIPE XIMENES BELO and JOSÉ RAMOS-HORTA	
	Introduction	3
	Announcement	5
	Presentation	7
	Biography of Carlos Filipe Ximenes Belo	13
	Nobel Lecture	15
	Biography of José Ramos-Horta	25
	Nobel Lecture	28
	Selected Bibliography	46
1997	INTERNATIONAL CAMPAIGN TO BAN LANDMINES and JODY WILLIAMS	
	Introduction	49
	Announcement	51
	Presentation	53
	The International Campaign to Ban Landmines (ICBL)	59
	Nobel Lecture	62
	Biography of Jody Williams	71
	Nobel Lecture	73
	Selected Bibliography	80
1998	JOHN HUME and DAVID TRIMBLE	
	Introduction	85
	Announcement	89
	Presentation	91
	Biography of John Hume	97
	Nobel Lecture	99
	Biography of David Trimble	105
	Nobel Lecture	107
	Selected Bibliography	118
1999	MÉDECINS SANS FRONTIÈRES	
	Introduction	123
	Announcement	125

	Presentation	127
	Médecins Sans Frontières (Doctors Without Borders)	133
	Nobel Lecture	135
	Selected Bibliography	144
2000	KIM DAE-JUNG	
	Introduction	147
	Announcement	159
	Presentation	151
	Biography	157
	Nobel Lecture	159
	Selected Bibliography	165

Peace 1996

CARLOS FILIPE XIMENES BELO

and

JOSÉ RAMOS-HORTA

*for their work towards a just and peaceful solution
to the conflict in East Timor*

INTRODUCTION

The 1996 award is an example of how the Nobel Peace Prize may help further international peace. The world took little note in 1975 when Moslem Indonesia invaded its tiny neighbor, East Timor, newly freed from Portuguese colonial rule and in the following years subjected its Catholic population to brutal oppression. In presenting the prize to Bishop Belo, the Catholic Apostolic Administrator and spiritual leader of the East Timorese within the country, and to José Ramos-Horta, their international spokesman in exile, the Nobel Committee expressed its "hopes that this award will stir efforts to find a diplomatic solution based on the people's rights to self-determination."

In his address presenting the prize, Committee Chair Francis Sejersted, speaking as a historian, was indeed hopeful. While Indonesia considered its annexation as an historic fact, he said, "History has never established anything as a fact forever. History always moves on." Just forty years ago, in 1956, the Soviet Union crushed a popular uprising in Hungary, now Hungary was free. "There are forces in history more powerful than the strongest military force."

So it turned out, and the Nobel prize played a part. It gave worldwide publicity to the plight of the East Timorese and helped bring about such international support for them that after an economic crisis forced Indonesia's long-time ruler, President Suharto to resign, the new government agreed to a referendum in 1999. This enabled the East Timorese to establish their independence in 2002 after a period of transitional governance by the United Nations. Today Xanana Gusmão, the guerilla leader who in 1996 was in prison is president of the country, and Ramos-Horta is Minister of Foreign Affairs and Cooperation. Some of his compatriots hoped that Bishop Belo would succeed Gusmao as president, but he had never considered politics as his true calling. Even as Apostolic Administrator, he could not have distanced himself from the politics of the new republic. He resigned as Apostolic Administrator and, after recovering from a time of ill health, he prepared to serve as a missionary in the former Portuguese colony of Mozambique, an assignment about which he had dreamed ever since his youth.

As Bishop Belo declared in his address at the award ceremonies in Oslo, "I speak as a spiritual leader, not as a politician, which in fact, I am not." He explained that his vocation had evolved "to the grave responsibility of trying to apply my fallible self to the difficult task of providing moral leadership in a situation where almost no one is ever completely happy with my action." The Indonesian authorities felt that he was too critical of them, while the East Timorese, especially the young people, felt that he was not critical enough of the Indonesian army's repressive actions.

ANNOUNCEMENT

The Norwegian Nobel Committee has decided to award the Nobel Peace Prize for 1996, in two equal parts, to Carlos Filipe Ximenes Belo and José Ramos-Horta for their work towards a just and peaceful solution to the conflict in East Timor.

In 1975 Indonesia took control of East Timor and began systematically oppressing the people. In the years that followed it has been estimated that one-third of the population of East Timor lost their lives due to starvation, epidemics, war and terror.

Carlos Belo, bishop of East Timor, has been the foremost representative of the people of East Timor. At the risk of his own life, he has tried to protect his people from infringements by those in power. In his efforts to create a just settlement based on his people's right to self-determination, he has been a constant spokesman for non-violence and dialogue with the Indonesian authorities. Ramos-Horta has been the leading international spokesman for East Timor's cause since 1975. Recently he has made a significant contribution through the "reconciliation talks" and by working out a peace plan for the region.

In awarding this year's Nobel Peace Prize to Belo and Ramos-Horta, the Norwegian Nobel Committee wants to honour their sustained and self-sacrificing contributions for a small but oppressed people. The Nobel Committee hopes that this award will spur efforts to find a diplomatic solution to the conflict in East Timor based on the people's right to self-determination.

PRESENTATION

Speech by Francis Sejersted, Chairman of the Norwegian Nobel Committee. Translation of the Norwegian text.

Your Majesties, Presidents, Excellencies, Ladies and Gentlemen,

On behalf of the Norwegian Nobel Committee, may I extend to everyone a warm welcome to this year's Nobel Peace Prize ceremony. It is one hundred years to the day since Alfred Nobel died. A year earlier, he had drawn up his will, in which he determined that his considerable wealth should provide for annual awards of five prizes, three for science, one for literature, and one for peace, to those whose work, as he wrote, "shall have conferred the greatest benefit on mankind." It was also laid down in the will that the Peace Prize should be awarded in Norway by a committee appointed by the Norwegian Storting. Our thoughts today go also to Stockholm, where the other awards are being made, and where the centenary is being marked of the death of Alfred Nobel.

Nobel was, of course, an unusually successful businessman. But that was not where his heart lay. His happiest times were spent in the laboratory. Inventions, it has been said, became for him a way of life. He was also very widely read. He was in other words greatly interested, indeed a believer, in science and literature. What was remarkable was his moral approach to those activities, which he saw as opportunities for promoting a better world. This perspective emerges most clearly in his decision concerning a peace prize. It can be argued that the invention of dynamite, and concern at the more powerful weapons which it made possible, contributed to his increasing commitment to peace. But there were other impulses, too, impulses which appealed to his deeply rooted moral instincts, first and foremost his contact with the future Peace Prize Laureate Bertha von Suttner and with the contemporary peace movement.[1]

Nobel left an important inheritance, consisting of a vision of a better world, and an award institution which was to contribute to the realisation of that vision. We who have been entrusted with managing that inheritance do so in humility and with deep respect for the man Alfred Nobel, whose memory we honour today.

It is with great pleasure, and in the conviction that with this year's choice we have managed Nobel's inheritance in the best possible way, that we welcome our Peace Prize Laureates today. Carlos Filipe Ximenes Belo and José Ramos-Horta have been awarded the Nobel Peace Prize for 1996 for their long-lasting efforts to achieve a just and peaceful solution to the twenty-year-old conflict in East Timor. To reach this peaceful winterland Norway, you have come about as far from your home country as it is possible to travel on this earth. Yet the distance between us is much shorter in miles than in opportunities for peace, justice and reconciliation. We are grateful and proud that, in the middle of your important and self-sacrificing work, you have found time for the journey here, thereby giving us this opportunity to honour you.

The conflict in East Timor has been called "the forgotten conflict." It has not, however, been completely forgotten, having figured on the international agenda, with varying degrees of prominence, throughout those twenty years. But it has so to speak never caught on. There have been so many other interests and regards to attend to, and East Timor is so small. Rarely has the cynicism of world politics been more clearly demonstrated. The numerous considerations of "Realpolitik" have enabled an exceptionally brutal form of neocolonialism to take place. Of a population of between six and seven hundred thousand, nearly two hundred thousand have died as the direct or indirect result of the Indonesian occupation. And the violations are still taking place today. Many are the countries which have given higher priority to their "Realpolitical" cooperation with Indonesia than to regard for East Timor. This is the apparently hopeless situation in which our two Laureates have so untiringly striven for a just and peaceful arrangement for their people.

The autumn of 1975 was fateful for East Timor. First the old colonial masters, the Portuguese, withdrew. Then an internal struggle broke out between the Timorese Democratic Union on the one hand and the Fretilin liberation movement[2] on the other. And the autumn ended with the Indonesian invasion. In the twenty-one years that have passed since, this conquest of a country and a people has never been internationally recognised. Ramos-Horta was a Fretilin leader, one of the moderates whose ideal was social democracy. During the so-called civil war, he was out of the country, and on his return in September he tried to reconcile the parties. Since the invasion he has lived abroad, unceasingly and with great personal sacrifice collecting and communicating information on the repression, torture and killing in his home country, and acting as East Timor's principal international spokesman. At the same time he has successfully kept up his efforts to unite the various East Timorese groups in a single national front, while constantly seeking opportunities for a peaceful solution to the conflict with Indonesia, based on respect for the integrity of the East Timorese people. "We used to joke that he was more an informal member of the Democratic Union than a Fretilin leader," says Union leader João Carrascalão. The remark illustrates the part played by Ramos-Horta as a mediator and conciliator. No serious negotiations aimed at resolving the conflict are conceivable today without the participation of Ramos-Horta or one of his aides, as Bishop Belo has also emphasised.

As a relatively unknown priest, Bishop Belo was appointed Apostolic Administrator for the Roman Catholic church in East Timor in 1983, since when he has served on his home ground. Again and again, in the midst of everyday terror and suffering, he has intervened, trying to reconcile and mediate and lessen confrontation, and in doing so he has saved many lives. Intervening in a violent conflict entails a risk of being crushed between the antagonists. "Pray for me, please," he said in one such situation, "because now I have to defend myself on both sides." But Bishop Belo has become much more than a mediator: this man of peace has also become a rallying point for his sorely tried people, a representative of their hope for a better future. The love his people feel for this mediator springs from certain fundamental principles he has adhered to. Show the people respect. Give them freedom to develop their humanity to the full. Then ask them whether they want to be Indonesians, Portuguese, or independent. Bishop Belo shares with his people the insight of the oppressed, an insight deeper than that of generals or oppressors. Why all this brutality? It does not even serve its purpose. You do not gain respect if you do not show respect.

This year has seen the commemoration, forty years on, of the Soviet Union's brutal crushing of the popular rising in Hungary in 1956. The West did not intervene. Since Hungary lay within the Soviet sphere of interest, it was necessary "Realpolitik" to accept the invasion. We would do well to recall that at that time, a marking of the event forty years later in a free Hungary lay beyond the bounds of what most people thought possible. It has been said that Indonesia's annexation of East Timor is a historic fact. But history has never established anything as a fact forever. History always moves on. If we have learned anything in the past decade, it must be that the most repressive regimes are the most fragile. There are forces in history more powerful than the strongest military force. Violence and terror do not lead to peace. Not until one builds up the courage to break out of the vicious circle of violence do opportunities arise for an enduring peace.

The right to live, the right to full development as human beings, the right to respect, are at the heart of the concept of human rights. Since the award of the Nobel Peace Prize for 1960 to Albert Lutuli,[3] work for human rights has been one of the principal criteria for the award. We have constantly received confirmation that this was the right path to take, although the choice of this criterion has also been criticised because it allegedly has nothing to do with peace. But it is precisely in forging a close link between the human rights criterion and peace that we believe we are realising that criterion's most universal and most fundamental aspects. Peace, stability and harmony must be based on mutual respect. That, so simple and so universal, is the message. Once it has been heard, the next step is to institutionalise the respect, in various ways according to cultural traditions. Violence, on the other hand, systematic violence on the part of those in power, can never be justified within the framework of a universal concept of human rights. That is a fact to which the victims of violence could testify. Never forget to listen to the voice of the victims, the voice of the nearly two hundred thousand whose lives were lost in massacres or from the hunger and want which resulted from the Indonesian invasion of East Timor.

This year's two Peace Prize Laureates, Carlos Filipe Ximenes Belo and José Ramos-Horta, have laboured tirelessly, and with great personal sacrifice, for their oppressed people. Under extremely difficult conditions, they have preserved their humanity and faith in the future. It is in admiration of their work and in the hope for a better future for East Timor that the Norwegian Nobel Committee today honours them with the Nobel Peace Prize for 1996.

CARLOS FILIPE XIMENES BELO

Born: Baucau, East Timor, 3 February 1946
Parents: Domingos Baptista Filipe
         Ermelinda Baptista Filipe

Education and Religious Training

East Timor
  1958   First Communion
  1958–   Elementary School: Salesian school at Ossu
  1963–68   Secondary School: Jesuit Seminary of St. Francis Xavier, Dare
  1968, October–   Leaves for Portugal

Portugal
  1969–70   Salesian Seminary at Mogofores. Last two years of high school.
  1971–72   Salesian Seminary at Manique do Estoril
  1973   Novitiate, Salesian Order
  1973–75   Philosophy studies: Instituto Superior de Estudios Teologicos, Lisbon
  1974   Accepted into Salesian Order
                    September. At supper in Casa Don Bosco, Salesian center in Lisbon, declares, "I am ready to become engaged in the process of building East Timor."

East Timor
  1974–75   Pastoral Orientation Year: teaching, Colegio de Fatumaca, Salesian (technical college)

Macau
  1975–76   Teaching. Colegio dom Bosco, Salesian College

Lisbon
  1976–79   Theological Studies: 1976–79 Universidade Catolica Portuguesa

Rome
1979–81   Bachelor in Theology Salesian Pontifical University Licentiate in Pastoral Theology, specialising in Spirituality

Lisbon
1981, July 26   Ordination to Priesthood

East Timor
1981, July   Returned
1981–83   Worked at Fatumaca College, Baucau
1983   *March.* Appointed Director, Fatumaca College
May. Elected Apostolic Administrator of Dili Diocese
October 13. Speaks out in church about "arrests and violence"
1988, June 19   Consecrated Bishop of Dili Diocese (titular Bishop of Lorium)
1989   *February.* Writes to United Nations Secretary General, asking for East Timor Referendum: "We are dying as a people and a nation."
October. Visit of Pope John Paul II to Dili
1990   Ad Limina visit to Rome. Has Papal audience. Visits Salesians in Spain.
1991   *July.* Second secret meeting with Xanana Gusmão, leader of East Timorese Resistance.
November 12. Massacre at Santa Cruz cemetery. Belo tries to give sanctuary to students seeking refuge.

Bishop Belo's letter to the UN marks a continuing public stand criticizing the violations of the human rights of the Timorese by Indonesian authorities. Through pastoral letters and numerous media interviews Belo calls for more humane treatment of his people. The Indonesians pressure him to discontinue these activities, and he receives threats of assassination. Pope John Paul is personally supportive of Bishop Belo, but the Catholic Church in Indonesia is interested in placating the Indonesian government in Jakarta, and there are those in the Vatican hierarchy who would favor this position.

Editorial note: As Bishop Belo did not submit a resumé, this biographical note has been based mainly on the biography of Bishop Belo by Arnold S. Kohen, to whom the editor is much indebted for his general assistance.

NOBEL LECTURE

December 10, 1996

by

CARLOS FILIPE XIMENES BELO

Your Majesties, Dear Members of the Norwegian Nobel Committee, Honorable Prime Minister, Excellencies, Ministers, Members of Parliament, Members of the Diplomatic Corps, Regarded Friends, Distinguished Guests, Friends, Ladies and Gentlemen,

"Nations will proclaim his wisdom, the assembly will celebrate his praises. If he lives long, his name will be more glorious than a thousand others, and if he dies, that will satisfy him rest as well."[4] (The Wisdom of Sirach, 39, 10–11)

Excellencies, Ladies and Gentlemen, I start with this biblical passage from the Book of Wisdom because it expresses with deep significance the memory of the man we remember this day whose esteemed Peace Prize bears his name. Today, the 10th of December, we celebrate the centennial anniversary of the death of a wise benefactor of humanity, a peace worker, Alfred Nobel.

Men of competence will never be extinguished from the memory of humanity because his wisdom, his dedication to the improvement of humanity, his tenacity for the progress of science in favor of mankind, makes people everywhere, all believers, all ideologies, feel in one way or another under an obligation to his talents and his boldness.

These men of competence are constantly disturbing the consciences of those who do not attend to the improvement of humanity. For it is a matter of fact that everyone should contribute in any way or form so that mankind become more and more humane.

What reasons, brought the Catholic Bishop of East Timor to be here in the presence of this assembly? I come from a social context that is already known to your Excellencies, where, due to circumstances, the aspirations and desires of the people are limited.

Taking the words from Terentius: *"Homo sum; humani nihil a me alienum puto."* (Terentius 1, 1,25)[5]

As man, as human being, I cannot remain indifferent in face of what concerns man.

As a member of a people, I have to share the destiny of the people, taking upon myself completely this mandate, knowing the risks that such an attitude will involve. Striving for the defense of the rights of all peoples is not only the privilege of those guiding the destiny of the people or those enjoying lofty positions in society, but it is the duty of everyone whatever rank or status. As a member of the Church, I take upon myself the mission of enlightening and the denouncing of all human situations which are in disagreement with the Christian concept and contrary to the teaching of the Church concerning all mankind.

The Catholic Bishop is a pastor of a part of God's people. His specific mission is spiritual. Such a mission is incumbent upon him basically as a dispenser of spiritual resources for the salvation of persons and for consolidating them in faith in Jesus Christ.

But mankind is not limited to a spiritual dimension, one should be saved as a whole, human and spiritual. In this aspect, any Catholic Bishop shall never be indifferent when a people's possibilities for human realization, in all dimensions, are not respected.

So the Nobel Peace Prize, attributed to a Catholic Bishop, is not homage to one person but also basically the gratitude for the encouragement that the Catholic Church has developed over the centuries in defense and promotion of the rights of human beings.

The teachings of the Second Vatican Council in Gaudium et Spes states: *"The Church thinks that she will respond to the deep desires of peoples, showing its final hope, preaching freedom, dignity of conscience and rights, that is just, in God's plan of salvation."*[6]

The duty given to the Church is not socio-political in nature but religious. And thus it is characteristic of the Church, a wellspring of enlightenment and energy, to empower and contribute to the strengthening of human society.

It is known to your Excellencies, the efforts of the Church concerning the suffering of the people of East Timor over the last twenty-one years. As Bishop of this people, I regard the Nobel Peace Prize not as something to merely esteem one person but as the rightful homage for the work done by the Catholic Church in East Timor, defending the inalienable rights of her people.

"Yet you have made him little less than a god, you have crowned him with glory and beauty." (Psalms, 8,5)

For the composer of this psalm, human dignity is taking root in his divine vocation, created by God.

This is my belief and knowledge about mankind which guides me and impels me as my conscience considers how I should act.

However, addressing this distinguished Assembly with beliefs and concepts about mankind may be quite humanistic. But I do believe for sure that among us we have something in common, that is we affirm that the human being is the subject of all concept and human activities. We declare that one's value and dignity does not depend on the individual's belief, religion, politics, philosophy, race or color of skin.

Man is a being for freedom. It means that one's realization is complete when capable to decide about one's options and taking responsibility for his or her actions without any kind of intimidation.

Man is a being realised in a community. It means that the social and ethnic group one belongs to is the background for his or her fulfillment.

Man is a being realized when there is a reciprocity of respect. It means that wherever human beings are not respected in their elementary rights by those in charge or by those responsible in society, as a consequence, we have oppression, slavery, arrogance, arbitrariness, death of individuals and death of a people.

Ladies and Gentlemen, these principles are valid for everybody and they are valid for the Church who also affirms that human dignity is rooted and fulfilled in God Himself.

Persons have been placed in society by God the Creator, but over and above this, each person is called to be united with Him as children of God and participating in God's happiness.

Moreover, the Church teaches that if this divine Foundation and the hope for eternal life are missing, human dignity is strongly damaged (Gaudium et Spes, 21).

The Catholic Church proclaims Jesus Christ as the great deliverer for all mankind. Indeed, Jesus frees each one from every moral and social slavery, giving back his or her true dignity as a human being.

In making Christ known, the Church reveals to everyone their true situation and calling, since Christ is the head and model of that renewed humanity imbued with that fraternal love, sincerity and spirit of peace, to which everyone aspires (Vatican II, AG. 8).

Your Majesties, Members of the Nobel Committee, my friends from around the world, I am profoundly honored to be before you today to receive the Nobel Prize for Peace. But whatever personal compliment I may receive, I believe that I have received this high tribute not because of who I am or what I have done. I firmly believe that I am here essentially as the voice of the voiceless people of East Timor who are with me today in spirit, if not in person. And what the people want is peace, an end to violence, and respect for their human rights. It is my fervent hope that the 1996 Nobel Prize for Peace will advance these goals.

Above all, above all else, I am mindful and humble in my thoughts of Pope John Paul II, who did so much in the face of overwhelming odds in the epochal struggle to remove the yoke of communism from Poland and other nations who have been told to be realistic and accept their fate. The Holy Father has provided an example and a depth of inspiration to me that can never be equaled. My gratitude to John Paul II cannot be adequately expressed.

I also think of others, especially from Asia who have never stood here. I contemplate with unending amazement the work of Mahatma Gandhi and his creed of non-violence in the movement for change. I think of China, and I pray for the well-being of Mr. Wei Jing Sheng[7] and his colleagues, and hope that they will soon be liberated from their jail cells, just as Indonesian leaders once were freed from the infamous Boven Digul prison after long years of cruel captivity. Surely, these same Indonesian leaders had earned a place here in Oslo even before I was born in 1948, at the height of their battle for freedom and dignity. I think of the fearless Indonesian fighters and I realize that history has so much to teach us if we would only take time to contemplate its richness.

I stand humbled in the august presence of my predecessors in this place here in Oslo. I think of The Reverend Dr. Martin Luther King Jr., "standing on the mountaintop, looking out at the promised land."[8] These words remind me of the view of the majestic mountains in my beloved East Timor — Mount Matabean (the Mountain of the Dead), near where I was born in the east; and Mount Ramelau in the west. As I look at these mountains in my frequent journeys throughout my native land, I feel ever more strongly that it is high time that the guns of war are silenced in East Timor, once and forever, it is high time that tranquillity is returned to the lives of the people of my homeland, it is high time that there be authentic dialogue. All people of goodwill must use every peaceful means of human ingenuity and intelligence to find ways to create a genuine peace based on mutual respect and human dignity.

East Timor is hardly alone in its search for peace and dignity, and it is of great importance to acknowledge the work of others. Last year I was privileged to be the guest in Belfast, Northern Ireland, of the 1976 laureate, Mrs. Mairead Corrigan Maguire,[9] whose increasing work for peace has touched many throughout the world. Mrs. Maguire graciously gave me an informative and moving tour of the troubled areas in Belfast, the night after many vehicles had been burnt in protest over the early release of a soldier convicted of killing an 18 year old girl. I pray that the people of Northern Ireland may know genuine peace, justice and tranquillity in the near future.

Last year, I met with His Holiness, Dalai Lama, and was deeply moved by his wisdom and kindness. The people of Tibet are never far from my prayers, nor are the communities of the indigenous peoples of the world who are increasingly being overwhelmed by aggressive modernity that presumes to call itself civilization.

I pray for peace in the Middle East and Afghanistan, which cannot be forgotten, and for the continuation of the peace process in Central America. And no human being can be indifferent to the drama in the Great Lakes area, in Burundi and Rwanda, and also Zaire, where human suffering cries out for a solution.

In South Africa, the search for peace deepens. For me the work of Archbishop Desmond Tutu is a shining example of the way truth can be combined with the quest for human rights, the way humor and humility can be mixed with righteousness, and I only pray that I may be worthy of his mantle. In Burma, I salute the strength and grace of Daw Aung San Suu Kyi, and pray that a better day may soon arrive for her and all her people.[10] May the beauty of music from her piano soften the hearts of armies and nations. In Burma and throughout the world, in places known and not well known, let us apply the words in the fifth chapter of Amos of the Old Testament: "Let Justice roll down like waters."

And let us always think of many anonymous people throughout the world, struggling for the protection of human rights. Day by day, working to convince the international community of the justice of their cause, whether they be Moslems or Christians, Protestants or Catholics, Hindus or Buddhists whether they be followers of age-old traditional beliefs, believers or nonbelievers. I say: press on, take courage, remain true to your ideals, you will not be forgotten.

The world censures those who take up arms to defend their causes and calls on them to use non-violent means in voicing their grievances. But when a people chooses the non-violent path, it is all too often the case that hardly anyone pays attention. It is tragic that people have to suffer and die and the television cameras have to deliver the pictures to people's homes everyday before the world at large admits there is a problem. Therein lies the enormous significance and the brave wisdom of the decision of the Nobel Committee to focus on East Timor this year; it represents the extraordinary recognition of East Timor's quest for peace and the recognition of its pleas for an end to suffering.

I speak of these things as one who has the responsibility to bear witness to what I have seen and heard, to react to what I know to be true, to keep the flame of hope alive, to do what is possible to warm the earth for still another day. I speak as a spiritual leader, not as a politician, which in fact, I am not. In recent weeks, some articles have described me as "a former shepherd," not realizing that my vocation only evolved from a boyhood job of tending water buffaloes to the grave responsibility of trying to apply my fallible self to the difficult task of providing moral leadership in a situation where almost no one is ever completely happy with my actions.

Others have written that if there had not been a war in East Timor, I would be spending all my time tending to the needs of troubled youth, which is the special calling of my religious order, The Salesians of St. John Bosco.[11] But this is only a matter of degree: Even now, I spend an overwhelming amount of energy in listening to and counseling the youth of East Timor, who urgently need such help because of their history. This is my special obligation, and one which I welcome.

Thus I must press on, aware of all the tasks that are far from complete. St. John Bosco once said that we will have the chance to rest in the hereafter, not in this world. And my life in the past thirteen years since I took up the post in East Timor illustrates the accuracy of Don Bosco's judgement in this regard among others. But my own hard work forms only a small part of what is necessary; the participation of others is vital. I extend the hand of friendship and goodwill to all those who provide genuine assistance or moral support in the vital struggle for peace in East Timor, throughout Asia, Africa, in the Western Hemisphere, throughout Europe, in Bosnia and elsewhere in the Balkans. Everywhere.

I must also praise the United Nations for its painstaking efforts on the question of East Timor, which have been of central importance in keeping the issue alive over many long years. In the face of great obstacles, in spite of all the difficulties, the United Nations have continued to persevere in the interest of generating dialogue that might one day create a lasting structure of peace in East Timor, and in many other places throughout the world.

There is no institution that can take the place of the United Nations, especially in the light of the history and credibility of the world organization. We cannot overlook the fact that the United Nations played an important role from its earliest days in the 1940's in assisting the struggle of Indonesia's nationalist movement. The young Indonesian Republic fought alone, with supreme courage, against the brute force of colonialism and its allies, ultimately receiving the indispensable moral backing that the new world association alone was able to provide. In the face of the moral weight of the United Nations, the Dutch and their allies could not carry on military operations with impunity, as other colonial powers did before the UN was formed in 1945. This must never be forgotten. Thus, the world must do whatever possible to strengthen the United Nations in the months and years ahead, in the deepest interests of all the peoples of the world.

Let it be stated clearly that to make peace a reality, we must be flexible as well as wise. We must truly recognize our own faults and move to change ourselves in the interest of making peace. I am no exception to this rule! Let us banish anger and hostility, vengeance and other dark emotions, and transform ourselves into humble instruments of peace.

People in East Timor are not uncompromising. They are not unwilling to forgive and overcome their bitterness. On the contrary, they yearn for peace, peace within their community and peace in their region. They wish to build bridges with their Indonesian brothers and sisters to find ways of creating harmony and tolerance.

Mutual respect is the basis of compromise. Let us start by making a sincere effort to change the very serious human rights situation in East Timor. The Church has played its part. We have formed a Justice and Peace Commission that is always ready to cooperate with the authorities to address problems.

Independent human rights officials have repeatedly visited East Timor and have recommended what needs to be done. As a first step, the release of

East Timor political prisoners has to be given urgent attention, in accordance with the section on Humanitarianism in the Panca Sila, The Five Principles of Indonesia's State Ideology.[12] Such a step would help create an important opening on the road to peace.

Ladies and Gentlemen, taking the liberty to remind you, in this Assembly, of my predecessor's appeal, Israel's former Prime Minister, the late Mr. Itzaak Rabin, speaking in New York, when the first historical meeting with President Arafat took place, he said: *"Stop bloodshed."*[13]

Making mine this same appeal, I say: *"Stop bloodshed."* And I add: Stop oppression. Stop violence. Stop conflict. Let us sit down around a table and understand each other, because we cannot tolerate extending for a long time the suffering of the people of East Timor. I think this is the fundamental intention of the Nobel Committee in awarding to us the prize, expressed on behalf of its president, Mr. Francis Sejersted.

Ladies and Gentlemen, East Timor was given the possibility to be heard through the voice of her two sons resounding throughout the world through this solemn assembly; but I would like that this attention shown by the world to East Timor be given the same intensity concerning the many other problems distressing other people.

There are similar situations, throughout the world, where people live under horrible conditions as Timor, but they have no possibility to be heard.

Daily, we get in our homes, news and images of suffering, pain destruction caused by war. *"War, this monster,"* as Father Antonio Vieira states, *"what it is doing, even God is not secure in the altar."*

I appeal to all men of goodwill and particularly those holding power to find solutions to these numberless conflicts. Solutions based on justice and solidarity, in order that fundamental rights can be respected.

I appeal, as well, to all professionals of the information media, charged with this great mission, that they regulate communication between all latitudes of the globe, doing it with a sense of truth and immunity for building up a society more humane and more just, without tendentious manipulation.

I would like, before I finish, to address some words to the youth around the world, particularly to the youth of my dear Timor: "Society is a succession of interwoven rings in which each generation has the duty to contribute to the next generation in order to live in the world peacefully fraternally. On your shoulders, dear young people of the entire world, weigh the responsibility to transform tomorrow's world into a society where peace, harmony and fraternity reign."

Dear youth, I quote from memory the great Indian poet Rabindranath Tagore: *"Youth, as a lotus flower, flourish just once in life."* Do not let it wither on the way.

Finally, an event is never a lonely action. The awarding of the Nobel Peace Prize to these two sons of Timor, Dr. José Ramos-Horta and myself has come about because many people groups and institutions have worked hard so that this event could become a reality.

At this moment I would like, in the first place, to thank the King and Queen of Norway, for being susceptible to the suffering of the people of East Timor, and for their generous presence in this solemn assembly.

My thanks goes to the Nobel Peace Prize Committee for their kind attention and courageous dedication on behalf of the plight of the East Timorese.

To the government and members of the Norwegian Parliament I thank you for the decision to honor us with the Nobel Peace Prize.[14]

I emphasize a little to thank Portugal and other friendly nations, as well as distinguished personalities who have proposed our names as candidates for the Nobel Peace Prize.

To the Timorese, here and abroad, I convey my indescribable gratitude and my communion and silent solidarity with you.

To His Holiness, Pope John Paul II, who has been persistent and attentive in following the situation and the suffering of the people and the Church in East Timor, I submit my filial devotion and the promise of unending fidelity and unity with Christ.

To the Pontifical Commission of Justice and Peace, particularly in the person of its President, His Eminence Cardinal Roger Etchegaray,[15] who had an opportunity to be in direct contact with the Church of Timor, I submit my deep gratitude.

I cannot forget the contribution of friends from other religions who, with discretion and fearless activity have made it possible for the Nobel Peace Prize for 1996 to be attributed to the Catholic Church in East Timor.

It would be unjust to forget, although I am aware that it is difficult to count the various Non Governmental Organizations, Humanitarian Groups, Church-related Groups and individuals who have worked hard, in silence and without much publicity, so that the Timorese can receive assistance and to ensure that the Timorese issue would not be buried under the dust of oblivion. With them, I share my happiness.

And finally, my sincere thanks to all the members of the social communication industry from all over the world. They have lent their voices in making known to the world the anguish and the suffering of the Timorese. I would like to pay my tribute to those who provide information about Timor, who risk their lives, some of them falling in East Timor's soil.

The Creator and Father of everything and all peoples will reward all of us and will give us strength, wisdom and courage to struggle for our fellow human beings because *"each one is the image and the likeness of God."* (Gen. 1,26)[16]

JOSÉ RAMOS-HORTA

Personal data
Date and place of birth: 26 December 1949, Dili, East Timor
Marital status: Divorced
Children: One son
Normal residence: Dili
Passport: European Union (Portuguese)

Current positions
- Senior Minister, Minister for Foreign Affairs and Cooperation, First Constitutional Government of East Timor
- Visiting Professor, Faculty of Law, University of New South Wales, Sydney
- Distinguished Visiting Professor, Victoria University, Melbourne

Other active positions
- Acting president, Uma Fukun, East Timor Cultural Centre, Dili
- Member of the Nobel Peace Commission on Arms Control
- Co-President, State of the World Forum, San Francisco, California
- Founder, lecturer and member of the Board of Directors, Diplomacy and Human Rights Program, Faculty of Law, University of New South Wales, Sydney
- Member of the Board of Directors, INTERNEWS, San Francisco, California
- Founder and main benefactor, "JRH Micro-Credit Program for the Poor"
- Honorary Chairman, Timor Aid, Dili, East Timor
- Advisory Board, International Service for Human Rights, Geneva
- Advisory Board, Counterpart International, Washington, DC

Major international awards
2000 – Gold Medal of the President of Italy
1999 – First Hague Peace Appeal Award
1998 – Gold Medal of the University of Coimbra
1998 – The Grand Cross of the Order of Freedom, President of Portugal
1997 – Medal of the University of San Francisco
1996 – Nobel Peace Prize, Oslo
1996 – First UNPO Freedom Prize, The Hague

1995 – International Peace Activist Award, Gleitsman Foundation, California
1993 – Professor Thorolf Rafto Human Rights Award, Bergen

Previous positions
(1969–1974)
– Reporter, editor, photojournalist
– Radio announcer, TV correspondent
– Secretary for Foreign Affairs and Information, ASDT (Timorese Social Democratic Association) (1974–1975)

(1975–1986)
– Minister for External Relations and Information, RDTL (1975–76)
– FRETILIN Representative to the United Nations and the US (1976–1990)
– Media Adviser to the government of Mozambique based in Washington (1986–87)

Academic background
– Diploma, Executive Program for Leaders in Development, Harvard University (1998)
– Master of Arts in Peace Studies, Antioch University, USA (1984)
– Senior Fellow in International Relations, St. Antony's College, Oxford University (1987)
– Post-graduate courses in American Foreign Policy at Columbia University (1983)
– Public International Law, the Hague Academy of International Law (1984)
– International Human Rights Law, the International Institute of Human Rights, Strasbourg, France (1984)
– Diploma in Advanced Studies in Public Relations, International Centre for Marketing (1973)
– Senior High School and elementary school in East Timor (1969)

Doctor Honoris Causa
– Doctor of Laws, Pontífica Universidade Católica, Campinas, São Paulo, Brazil (1996)
– Doctor of Laws, Antioch University, Yellow Springs, Ohio, USA (1997)
– Doctor of Laws, University of New South Wales, Sydney, Australia (1998)
– Doctor of Laws, Rutgers University, New Jersey, USA (2000)
– Doctor of Laws, University of Oporto, Portugal (2000)

- Doctor of Humane Letters, University of Nevada, Reno, USA (2000)
- Doctor of Laws, Sunshine Coast University, Queensland, Australia (2001)

Books and other writings
- FUNU: The Unfinished Saga of East Timor, Red Sea Press, Trenton, NJ (1987)
- TIMOR LESTE: Amanhã em Dili, Dom Quixote, Lisbon (1994). Translated into French, German, Norwegian
- East Timor and International Law (1984), MA Thesis, Antioch University, USA
- Opinion pieces published in the International Herald Tribune, Sydney Morning Herald, The Age, Australian, Guardian, Le Monde, Le Monde Diplomatique, Boston Globe, San Francisco Chronicle, Folha de São Paulo, etc.

Languages
Portuguese, Tetun, English, French, Spanish

Hobbies
Tennis, walking, horse riding, motorbike, novels, history books, biographies, movies, opera and classical concerts

P. O. Box 6
Dili
East Timor
jrhorta@attglobal.net
http://www.easttimor.com

NOBEL LECTURE

December 10, 1996
by
JOSÉ RAMOS-HORTA

Suas Majestades, Honoráveis Membros do Comité Nobel da Paz, Senhores Presidentes, Senhores Primeiros Ministros, Excelências,

Com vossa permissão as minhas primeiras palavras serão na língua de Camões, Fernanda Pessoa, Agostinho Neto, Jorge Amado, Xanana Gusmão.

Apesar da brutal colonização indonésia e da repressão cultural dos últimos 21 anos, da proibição de uma língua e cultura que chegaram à nossa região há cerca de 500 anos, em Timor Leste esta língua secular ainda persiste teimosamente.

Sendo o segundo timorense de nacionalidade portuguesa a ser honrado com o Prémio Nobel da Paz, o primeiro é o nosso respeitado e venerado bispo Dom Carlos Filipe Ximenes Belo, faltaria à minha herança histórica e consciência se não começasse esta minha intervenção na língua que hoje une mais de 200 milhões de pessoas nas cinco regiões do mundo.

É com um profundo sentimento de humildade que me associo aqui a Dom Carlos Filipe Ximenes Belo para receber o Prémio Nobel da Paz 1996 que foi outorgado ao povo de Timor Leste.

Registo a minha eterna gratidão àqueles que me propuseram para este prémio. Estou lhes para sempre moralmente endividado e asseguro que as modestas dádivas de saúde e inteligência que Deus me deu serão sempre postas ao serviço da paz e justiça para o meu povo e para a causa da paz, liberdade e democracia em todas as latitudes onde a minha fraca voz possa ser ouvida.

Apenas por razões práticas vou continuar a minha intervenção na língua inglesa.

I will now resume my speech in English

Your Majesties, Honourable Members of the Nobel Committee, Presidents, Prime Ministers, Excellencies,

With your permission, my first words will be in the language of Camões, Fernando Pessoa, Agostinho Neto, Jorge Amado and Xanana Gusmão.[17]

In spite of the brutal Indonesian colonisation and cultural repression of the past 21 years that attempted to eradicate a language and culture that reached our region almost 500 centuries ago, in East Timor this rich centuries-old language survives stubbornly.

Being the second East Timorese of Portuguese nationality to be honoured with the Nobel Peace Prize (the first is our respected and revered Bishop Carlos Filipe Ximenes Belo), I would be failing my own historical heritage and conscience if I were to start this Nobel lecture in another language other than in the language that unites more than 200 million people in the five regions of the world.[18]

It is with a deep feeling of humility that I join today with Bishop Carlos Filipe Ximenes Belo to receive the 1996 Nobel Peace Prize that has been bestowed on the people of East Timor.

My eternal gratitude to those who nominated me. I am forever morally indebted to, and I can assure them, that God's modest gifts of health and wisdom to me will always be put to the service of peace and justice not only for my country and people but also for the cause of peace, freedom and democracy everywhere where my faint voice can be heard.

My deepest appreciation goes to the Nobel Committee for having chosen us for the 1996 Nobel Peace Prize. Your generosity in thinking of the wretched of the earth, and your courage in standing up to the might of States, the cynicism and indifference of too many and betrayal by some, tells also a lot about the soul and history of courage of this great country of yours that fought bravely during World War II.

In recent years Norway has played a central role in fostering dialogue and peace among historical enemies. In the Middle East and Central America, your discreet nature, determination and creativity have proven that some of the world's seemingly intractable conflicts can be resolved when there is an honest mediator and when the parties in the conflict are willing to end the war.

Small countries like Norway, Costa Rica and Portugal, and others, can succeed in mediating conflicts when mighty powers failed. Diplomacy and mediation are not prerogatives of the major powers. The small and medium-size countries without ambitions to a neo-imperial role and whose strength is their moral integrity are best placed to open dialogue among the parties in a conflict.

The East Timorese Church
The real winner of the 1996 Nobel Peace Prize is our spiritual leader, Dom Carlos Filipe Ximenes Belo. He is the embodiment of the East Timorese people's resilience, moral rectitude, dignity and identity, and its long quest for peace and freedom. In Dom Carlos the people of East Timor have found spiritual comfort and some sense of security from the daily threats to their very existence.

The people of East Timor owe almost everything to their Church. Hence, the 1996 Nobel Peace Prize is a tribute to the whole church, the courageous priests, nuns and lay workers and the people of East Timor.

My share of the Nobel Peace prize will go entirely to a Foundation to be called Peace and Democracy Dom Martinho da Costa Lopes.[19] I know this is too small a tribute to this great man who gave his life to his church and people.

The solidarity movement
I would like also to express my gratitude to three organisations that in the past honoured my people with less well-known awards but with equal importance for our people. To Professor Thorolf Rafto Human Rights Foundation from Bergen, Gleitsman Foundation, from California, and the Un-Represented Nations and Peoples Organisation (UNPO) based in The Hague, goes my profound gratitude.

With the men, women and children in many parts of the world who have given us so many years of their lives I wish to share this moment of joy. Without the generous solidarity movement we would be even poorer and alone. Some of our good friends have passed away from this earth: Denis Freney, Michelle Turner, Michel Robert, Carlos Vilares, the little and beautiful Sarah Taylor whom God took away at age 15. We will remember them forever.

Angola, Cape Verde, Guinea-Bissau, Mozambique, São Tomé and Príncipe
My special greetings of friendship and eternal gratitude to my good friend, President Joaquim Chissano of Mozambique, for having taken the trouble to fly to Oslo to be with us.

You have been with us in our most lonely years when the rest of the world pretended we did not exist or offered us advice on how best to surrender. From this Noble rostrum I bow to your late predecessor, Samora Moisés Machel, one of the greatest men Africa has known.

My special greetings and deepest gratitude to presidents José Eduardo dos Santos of Angola, Mascarenhas Monteiro of Cape Verde, Nino Vieira of Guinea-Bissau, and Miguel Trovoada of São Tomé and Príncipe for their friendship and generosity.

Your peoples and countries have been with us through our lonely years and I believe that you will be with us still in the years to come.

To the people of Angola who have suffered beyond imagination and are still in a painful process of national reconciliation, I extend our solidarity and friendship.

Angola paid a heavy price for the liberation of Namibia and South Africa. Yet there has not been enough recognition of the enormous contribution that the two lusophone countries, Angola and Mozambique, gave to the liberation of Southern Africa.

Portugal
I wish to state from this august rostrum the eternal gratitude of the people of East Timor and my own to the people of Portugal, the President, our good friend Dr. Jorge Sampaio and his predecessor, Dr. Mário Soares, a man of principles and compassion.

Through Your Excellency, Mr. President, I humbly ask you to convey to your wonderful and generous people, members of Parliament and government, past and present, our most heartfelt appreciation for your gallant efforts in support of our struggle.

For many years you fought a lonely battle in the European Union against the indifference and even hostility of some of your partners. You have shown not only to us the East Timorese but to other smaller nations in the world that principles and morality have not been taken over completely by mercantile interests.

Brazil
I recently visited Brazil and was warmly welcomed by everyone. I humbly ask President José Sarney to convey to President Fernando Henrique Cardoso and through him to all the people of Brazil our admiration and affection for your great country and people. My warmest greetings to Betinho, Dom Paulo Evaristo and Dom Hélder Câmara, the conscience of the poor of Brazil and the world.

Your Majesties,
This speech belongs to someone else who should be here today. He is an outstanding man of courage, tolerance and statesmanship. Yet, this man is in prison for no crime other than his ideas and vision of peace, freedom and dignity of his people.

Xanana Gusmão, leader of the people of East Timor, remains incommunicado in a prison thousands of miles away from his country. His trial in 1993 was universally condemned as a charade and was no more valid than the Dutch imprisonment and trial of the late President Sukarno, founding father of the Indonesian Republic.

I bow to Xanana and through him to my good friends Nino Konis Santana, David Alex, Tahur Matan Ruak, Fernando Araújo and all East Timorese prisoners of conscience in jails in East Timor and Indonesia, to the thousands of victims of torture, widows and orphans. I bow to the memory of Sabalae and the thousands of our dead.

Through Xanana I bow to my people with profound respect, loyalty and humility because they are the martyrs, the real heroes and peace-makers.

The New Order regime and the Indonesian people
The East Timorese are not the exclusive victims of the Indonesian New Order regime installed in 1965.[20] For more than 30 years, the Indonesian people have known massacres, imprisonment, torture, bans on writers, journalists, academics and labour leaders. Moslems, Catholics, Buddhists and Hindus have all known their share of repression. The only non-discriminatory policy of the New Order regime is when it comes to repression.

I pay tribute to the many tens of thousands of Indonesians who died in their own struggle for freedom and democracy, who languished in the jails of the New Order, or were forced into exile in China, Albania, USSR and Western Europe. I met many of them over the years and shared long hours of conversation about our people's suffering and dreams.

The lessons of the Jewish holocaust
In 1939, a few months before the outbreak of World War II, Harry Truman read a passionate message from President Roosevelt to the "National Meeting for Moral Rearmament" held in Washington.

The same time as the conference delegates were listening and applauding President Roosevelt's moral speech, 900 Jewish refugees on a boat from Germany anchored off Florida were waiting for a decision from Washington as to whether they should find sanctuary in the US or be sent back.

Finally, word came that their application for refugee status had been denied. The desperate refugees did not convince the morally courageous delegates to the "National Meeting for Moral Rearmament" that they had a valid fear of persecution. The 900 men, women and children were sent back to Germany. Many ended up in Hitler's death camps.[21]

More than half a century after the Jewish holocaust and centuries after the genocide of the indigenous peoples of Australia and the Americas, the same attitude that has allowed these crimes to take place persists today.

Opinion-makers and leaders, academics, writers and journalists who pretend to be objective and neutral in the face of racism and discrimination, the rape of a small nation by a larger power, the persecution of a weaker people by a ruthless army must share the guilt. No amount of intellectual argument will suffice to erase their responsibility.

Synagogues are still being desecrated. Gypsies are still discriminated against. Indigenous peoples continue to see their ancestral land taken over by developers, their culture and beliefs, and their very existence reduced to a tourist commodity.

Like the Jews and Armenians in the past, like the Kurdish, Gypsies, Tibetans, Aborigines of Australia, Maoris of Aotearoa (New Zealand), Kanakis of New Caledonia, the peoples of Western Sahara, and the Indigenous peoples of the Americas, the East Timorese are a mere footnote of history, an expendable people.

Cold War footnote
The conflict in East Timor can be traced back to the political context of the Cold War.

You might recall a picture that made headlines in the spring of 1975. I refer to the picture of an American helicopter landing on the rooftop of the US Embassy in Saigon to rescue remaining diplomats, CIA operatives and a few privileged South Vietnamese stooges as Saigon fell to the Vietcong. Cambodia and Laos followed. This picture illustrated better than a thousand words the ignominious American retreat from Indochina.

In another continent, in the horn of Africa, the longest reigning US ally, emperor Hailé Selassie of Ethiopia, had been overthrown a year earlier by radical army officers. Further south, the Portuguese empire had collapsed. These events seemed to confirm Lyndon B. Johnson's domino theory which was the rationale for US intervention in Indochina.

It was in this geopolitical context that President Gerald Ford and his Secretary of State, Henry Kissinger, visited Jakarta in early December 1975 as part of an Asian tour to reassure leaders of the region that the US would continue to honour its security commitments in Asia.

The invasion of East Timor which took place within hours of Ford's departure from Jakarta was a mere footnote in the Cold War events of 1975. Thousands of East Timorese who died in the days, weeks, months and years that followed were mere footnotes to the post-Vietnam and Cold War.

Inviolability of colonial boundaries
One and a half years before these events, in June 1974, I visited Jakarta, in my capacity as Secretary for Foreign Affairs of the Timorese Social Democratic Association, that had just been created, less than a month earlier. I had the privilege of meeting with the then Foreign Minister of Indonesia, Mr. Adam Malik. After our third round of talks, Mr. Malik addressed to me a letter which read in part:

The independence of every country is the right of every nation, with no exception for the people of (East) Timor;

... whoever will govern in Timor in the future after independence can be assured that the government of Indonesia will always strive to maintain good relations, friendship and co-operation for the benefit of both countries.

The following year, in April 1975, I again visited Indonesia and met with President Suharto's senior adviser, General Ali Mortopo, to whom I reiterated our collective desire to develop friendly relations with Indonesia. General Mortopo reassured me that Indonesia harboured no territorial ambitions over East Timor. However, we soon learned that the word of an Indonesian general or diplomat can be broken as easily as it is spoken.

Some simple but fundamental issues need to be addressed. Does Indonesia have a valid historical claim to East Timor?[22]

The current boundary of the Republic of Indonesia is a product of the Dutch East Indies administration. West New Guinea was absorbed by the Republic not because of a reasonable historical, cultural, ethnic kinship or geographic continuity. The only link that justified the annexation was West New Guinea's brief colonisation by the Dutch.

The arbitrary carving up of Africa at the Berlin Conference[23] can be blamed for some of Africa's problems today but respect for the colonial boundaries, as unfair as most might be, has provided some peace and stability and kept most of Africa, Latin America and Asia from disintegrating.

Saddam Hussein of Iraq attempted to redraw the map and rectify what he perceived to be an unfair colonial legacy by invading Kuwait. Iran has longstanding claims over Bahrain. In Latin America there are some inter-state territorial disputes as a result of perceived unfair border delimitation.

The right of peoples to self-determination
From the Chittagon Hill Tracts in Bangladesh to Bougainville, Kurdistan, Sri Lanka, India, Tibet, Chechnya, Ogoni, West Papua, millions of peoples seek to assert their most fundamental rights and if we attempt to find a common denominator for the problems I have just listed there is one: the right of peoples to self-determination.

In most cases the demands are not for secession. They are about their survival as a people with a language and a culture, with their land and environment protected from rapacious multinationals. Only when these basic demands are not met has there been recourse to other forms of struggle with an escalation in their demands.

While self-determination in the de-colonisation process of the non-self-governing territories almost always led to independence, this is not the case in most of the conflicts of today. The cases of Western Sahara and East Timor, are the two most salient failures of decolonisation. In the case of Western Sahara, the UN has allowed itself to be a pawn in the machinations of a minor regional power.[24]

The preservation of the territorial integrity of a country can be achieved only if those in power are sensitive to the basic demands and aspirations of the many indigenous peoples and nationalities that make up the country.

Brute force might silence and keep dormant the dreams and aspirations of a people but the anger simmering for decades will inevitably resurface and break-up the country.

The right of the people of East Timor to self-determination
The right of the people of East Timor to self-determination is widely recognized. Apart from the former Spanish territory of Western Sahara, East Timor is the largest non-self-governing territory in the UN General Assembly decolonisation list which dates back to 1960.

The UN General Assembly and Security Council have adopted a total of 10 resolutions on the question of East Timor all reaffirming this right.

In its ruling of 30 June 1995 on the *Case Concerning East Timor, Portugal vs Australia,* the International Court of Justice stated that the right of self-determination has an *erga omnes* character and that the people of East Timor are entitled to it.

Dialogue without pre-conditions and the CNRM Peace Plan[25]
The Israeli-Palestinian peace talks and South Africa's transition to democracy give us renewed hope in that they demonstrate that seemingly intractable problems can be resolved if there is political will and vision by all involved.

In this room today there are East Timorese leaders of every persuasion, some have come all the way from East Timor, Portugal and Australia, and I can speak for all when I say that we are ready to enter into a process of dialogue with the Indonesian authorities, under the auspices of the United Nations, without pre-conditions, to explore all possible ideas towards a comprehensive settlement of the conflict.

In 1992, after thorough consultation with our people in the country, Xanana Gusmão gave his seal of authority to what is now known as the CNRM Peace Plan which was formally presented to a meeting of the European Parliament in Brussels on 22 April 1992.

The CNRM proposal remains valid as a modest contribution towards finding a solution to the conflict.

Phase One — Humanitarian phase
This phase which should take up to two years to be fully implemented, would involve all three parties working with the UN to implement a wide range of "confidence building measures", (GBMs) but would not deal with the core of the problem which is the issue of self-determination.

These CBMs must include release of all prisoners, end of torture and summary executions and a drastic reduction in Indonesia troop presence in the territory.

These are some of the ideas which I believe could be implemented immediately without loss of face for Indonesia. Its international standing would improve significantly and its presence in the territory would be less resented, thus relieving a very tense situation.

In view of the time constraints, the full text of this plan is attached to this speech.

Phase Two — Autonomy, 5 years
Phase two, lasting between five to ten years, would be a period of genuine political autonomy based on ample powers vested in a local, democratically elected Territorial People's Assembly.

At the end of the second phase, the autonomous status of the territory could be extended by mutual accord.

The East Timorese people, having enjoyed a period of peace and freedom without the presence of the most hated symbol of the occupation, the army, might accept to continue this form of association.

Conversely, the changing generation, attitudes and perception in Indonesia might result in Indonesia accepting as natural that East Timor becomes independent.

Phase Three — Self-determination
If all parties agree that Phase Three should enter into effect immediately, then the UN begins to prepare a referendum on self-determination to determine the final status of the territory.

If God willing, East Timor becomes independent, ladies and gentlemen, allow me to share with you, our vision for our country's future and role in the region.

Our vision for the future
East Timor is at the crossroads of three major cultures: Melanesian, which binds us to our brothers and sisters of the South Pacific region; MalayPolynesian binding us to Southeast Asia; and the Latin Catholic influence, a legacy of almost 500 years of Portuguese colonisation. This rich historical and cultural existence place us in a unique position to build bridges of dialogue and co-operation between the peoples of the region.

Portugal
East Timor will maintain close ties with Portugal, a country which colonized us for almost half a millennium has shown an abiding commitment to our right to self-determination. Portugal and East Timor will be most valuable partners for ASEAN in its relations with the EU, Africa and Latin America.

Australia and the South Pacific
The majority of the East Timorese residents outside the country are in Australia. In spite of our sadness over Australia's role on East Timor I wish to state here our deepest appreciation to Australia for the shelter, hospitality and generosity shown to the thousands of East Timorese refugees on Australian soil.

We appreciate the many representations the previous and current governments of Australia have made to impress upon the government of Indonesia regarding the human rights situation in East Timor. No other Western country has been more persistent in this regard.

We fought together during World War II and many East Timorese gave their lives for our common cause. Now and in the future, we look up to Australia for help. An independent East Timor will seek close relations with Australia and membership in the South Pacific Forum.

ASEAN and APEC[26]

We are conscious of our geography which compels us to co-exist with our neighbours in that part of the world. We will seek membership in ASEAN and APEC within days of our independence.

A Zone of Peace

We will not have a standing army. For our external security, we will rely on a Treaty of Neutrality to be guaranteed by the permanent members of the Security Council. We will endeavour with the UN and our neighbours to declare our region and the seas surrounding East Timor a Zone of Peace and Development.

Rule of Law

We will endeavour to build a strong democratic state based on the rule of law which must emanate from the will of the people expressed through free and democratic elections.

Human rights and international obligations

All international human rights treaties will be submitted to the Parliament for ratification.

We believe that human rights transcend boundaries and must prevail over state sovereignty.

We will introduce into the school curriculum at an early stage starting in the kindergarten the subject of human rights.

We will actively work with like-minded countries, NGOs and the media to strengthen the UN human rights machinery.

Amnesty and national reconciliation

East Timorese now serving in the Indonesian administration in East Timor, the security forces and police, should not fear an independent East Timor. They will be invited to stay on. Their full and active involvement in running the country will be necessary to insure a smooth transition.

Our society will not be based on revenge. Because of its credibility and standing, the Catholic Church will be expected to play a major role in the healing process of our society.

In August 1975, too many East Timorese died in brief but violent civil strife. Many more died even after the invasion because some in the leadership of the movement I belonged to, took upon themselves the role of judges and executioners.

National reconstruction and development
East Timor is a relatively small country. But with an area of 18,889 km^2 and a total population of 700,000 (1974 figures), it is at least equal to, if not larger, in size and population, than some 40 independent states. It is potentially self-sufficient in most agricultural goods, meat and fish. It has large reserves of oil, natural gas, marble and manganese.

The invasion up-rooted thousands of people. Properties were abandoned, destroyed or sold at unfair prices. This situation will be redressed. A voluntary resettlement plan will be effected to allow the many tens of thousands of displaced East Timorese to return to their ancestral lands. We believe in free education and health care for our people. The money saved from not having a standing army will be well used in these areas. With the co-operation of WHO we will seek to eradicate malaria, tuberculosis and other preventable diseases within a decade.

Indonesian migrants
It is estimated that over 100,000 Indonesians are now living in East Timor. Most are poor Indonesians who came to our country looking for a better life.

Indonesian migrants in East Timor will be welcome to stay.

The Suharto regime, its achievements and what it should do
No one can honestly suggest that the 30-year regime of General Suharto has not done good for Indonesia. The record of the past 20 years has been impressive. The Suharto regime lifted the Indonesian economy from extreme poverty to the status of an economic tiger. Living standards, literacy, health care and food production increased to impressive levels.

President Suharto can show leadership by releasing all prisoners, meeting Indonesia's greatest living author, Pramoedya Ananta Toer, Megawati Sukarnoputri, leader of the PDI,[27] daughter of Indonesia's founding father, the late Bung Karno, Muchtar Pakpahan, Indonesia's Lech Walesa, Sri Bintang, George Aditjondro, Indonesia's most decorated environmentalist.

The leaders and militants of the PRD are among the best children of Indonesia. Instead of hunting them he should invite them to his palace for dialogue about the future.

Fostering a democratic and peaceful transition in Indonesia
No country, no matter how rich and endowed with natural resources, is an island unto itself. In an increasingly smaller world and competitive age, where

modern electronic communications break the barriers of silence erected by dictators, Indonesia cannot continue to flout the right of the people of East Timor to self-determination and the rule of law in Indonesia.

The next two to three years will witness a transition in Indonesia. Australia, New Zealand, the US, Canada and the EU can encourage a peaceful, evolutionary transition with a discrete yet firm policy of pushing for democratic reforms and rule of law in Indonesia and for a genuine act of self-determination in East Timor.

The role of the international community
We are as determined as we are optimistic about our future. To Indonesia and our other neighbours in the ASEAN we are offering a hand of friendship and appealing to them to help us bring peace and freedom to East Timor.

The EU, working with the US, Canada, Australia, New Zealand, Japan and Indonesia's partners in ASEAN, can accelerate the on-going dialogue under the auspices of the UN Secretary-General, and give it some impetus and real substance.

The US Administration is the only major power that has adopted some concrete measures to encourage changes in Indonesia and East Timor. I express here our sincere appreciation to President Clinton for his actions on East Timor and I appeal to him to lend his youthful energy and compassion towards a permanent resolution of the conflict which he once described as "unconscionable."

The West and arms sales
We are not asking that Indonesia be punished with comprehensive economic sanctions. We believe that economic engagement with a country can at times foster positive changes through the development of a democratically conscious class.

However, we find it repulsive that the Western countries that more loudly make rhetorical speeches about human rights are the ones that manufacture most weapons that have killed more than 20 million people in the developing world since World War II.

Land mines, torture equipment, cluster bombs, chemical weapons are weapons designed to inflict pain and death on human beings. Most victims are civilians, women and children. How can arms manufacturers, weapons designers, plant managers, politicians, who have families of their own whom they love, be so insensitive when it comes to the suffering of other human beings?

Human rights and "Asian values"
The peoples of Burma, Thailand, the Philippines, South Korea, and the democracy movements in China and Indonesia are telling the rest

of the world that democracy and human rights are not an invention of the West.

The thousands of Asians who died in the streets of Manila, Bangkok, Jakarta, Rangoon, Beijing, did not die for a so-called "Asian value" that denies the people of Asia the basic and fundamental freedoms enjoyed in Europe, Latin America and in an increasing number of countries in Africa.

South Korea
The brave people of Korea who endured decades of dictatorship and occupation won the struggle for democracy not with guns but with their tenacity in fighting the troops in the streets of Seoul and Kwangju.

The South Korean people can also show greater courage by being magnanimous and forgive those who have done wrong. Sometimes in history individuals in power are driven to commit wanton crimes but those who survive and are in power today should resist the temptation to exact revenge in the name of justice.

The death sentence must be abolished and the brave people of Korea should set the example by commuting the death sentence on former President Chun Do Hwan. From here I appeal to my Korean friends not to exact revenge against those who have been defeated. In victory be magnanimous.

Burma
I extend our most heartfelt solidarity to the brave people of Burma and their elected leader, Nobel Peace Laureate Daw Aung San Suu Kyi, in their struggle for democracy, rule of law and human rights.

At a time when some ASEAN rulers are conniving with the SLORC regime[28] to deny the people of Burma their democratic victory, we must all stand up and redouble our efforts to restore democracy to Burma.

The US and the EU must be commended for their leadership in support of the restoration of democracy in Burma but they must escalate the pressure with additional diplomatic and economic sanctions against the SLORC.

I also fully endorse the recommendations on Burma adopted by the Forum of Democratic Leaders in the Asia Pacific led by Kim Dae-jung and Cory Aquino in their recent meeting in Manila.

China, Taiwan, Tibet
When the UN SC debated the issue of East Timor in 1975 and 1976 China was our closest ally. I worked closely with very able Chinese diplomats. In spite of the indifference of the other four permanent members, China, along with other non-permanent members, succeeded in pushing the SC to adopt two resolutions on East Timor.

It is with this feeling of gratitude and admiration for China that I appeal to the Chinese leaders to listen to their own people's opinions and desires for a more open society, based on the rule of law, democracy, and freedom of speech. These are after all rights that are granted to each Chinese citizen by their own Constitution.

Wei Jing Zhen is one of China's best children. He is being wasted away when his talents could best be used in the service of his fellow Chinese people and country.

The people of Taiwan have shown great maturity, responsibility and commitment to peace and democracy. While there is no dispute that Taiwan is part of China, as long as there is no progress on the issue of peaceful reunification of the two countries, I believe that the cause of dialogue and peace can best be served if Taiwan is granted observer status in the UN as was the case in the past with South and North Korea, South and North Vietnam. After all, China has not objected to Taiwan and Hong Kong joining the APEC.

China should listen to the voice of peace and moderation of the Tibetan people. For many years the Tibetan spiritual leader, His Holiness the Dalai Lama, has offered a moderate peace proposal to the Chinese authorities to settle the Tibetan conflict.

Cyprus
Cyprus, a shining example of democracy and tolerance, remains divided and occupied by a NATO ally whose history of aggression and violence is wellknown.

Recently I received a letter signed by the students of Classes C11 and C22 of Kykko B Lyceum in Nicosia who wrote:

Your homeland is an occupied country at the far end of the ocean. Our homeland lies partly occupied at the far end of the Mediterranean. We live in a divided city and we cannot cross the dividing line...

To the students of Kykko B Lyceum I can only say that like the ancient Armenia you too will recover your lost land.

The prophets of doom
The world has changed dramatically over the last few years and the theorists of irreversibility and *status quo* have been discredited by the collapse of the USSR.

Who would have thought it possible that the great Armenian people, persecuted for hundreds of years would regain a country called Armenia? The entire world conspired against the Eritrean people. Americans, Russians and Cubans all connived against that small nation. Two great nations, Israelis and Palestinians, who swore eternal hatred have shown courage and wisdom and began a painful process of dialogue. In South Africa, former enemies are trying to rebuild their common home.

Last but not least, for the prophets of doom, for those in government who counsel us "realism", allow me to remind them of a news item in the ever reliable BBC a few years ago.

It was sometime in early 1991 and I was driving from the small Swiss town of Nyon, to the Palais des Nations in Geneva, to yet another round of futility in a place where some diplomats pretend to be too busy to listen to real problems of real peoples.

The BBC was telling us the story of a Soviet cosmonaut who had gone into space a few months earlier on one of those record-breaking missions in space. When he was blasted off from somewhere in the Soviet Union he carried a passport and a nationality granted to him by the most feared military empire in the world.

Once he completed his tour of duty for the pride of the socialist motherland he prepared the spacecraft for its return voyage to earth. But he no longer had a country to return to. The mighty empire had ceased to exist. He was forced to circle the earth a few days longer until people of good will on earth decided to which country he should go to.

With this note, I will end with renewed hope that no matter the level of brute force used against us, our dreams will never die.

God bless you all. Thank you.

THE CNRM PEACE PLAN

Phase One (one to two years to be implemented)
The CNRM does not pretend that this plan is the only blue-print for a peaceful resolution of the East Timor conflict. However, it believes that it at least can be the basis for discussion by all parties.

This phase of the talks must focus on achieving:

Immediate end to all armed activities in East Timor;
Reduction of Indonesian troop presence to a maximum of 1000 within a six-month period;
Removal of all heavy weapons, tanks, helicopters, combat aircraft, long-range artillery;
Immediate and unconditional release of all political prisoners;
Reduction by 50 per cent of Indonesian civil servants in East Timor;
Stationing in the territory of UN Specialised Agencies such as UNICEF, UNDP, WHO, FAO;
A comprehensive census of the population;
Establishment of an independent Human Rights Commission under the Catholic Bishop;
Lifting of all media control by the army;
Freedom of political activities;

*Removal of restrictions on the teaching of Portuguese; a Portuguese Cultural Institute is set up;
*Appointment of a resident representative of the UN Secretary-General.

Phase Two — Autonomy phase (5 to 10 years)
Full implementation of phase one is a pre-requisite for the successful implementation of phase two. Elections for a Territorial Assembly will be free and fair only if they are conducted after the full implementation of phase one.

The following must be implemented in the second phase:
*Political parties, including those advocating independence for East Timor, are legalised;
*The EU sets up a legation in East Timor headed by a senior Portuguese official;
*Elections are held for a Territorial Assembly. The UN to provide technical support and supervision of the entire process;
*Only Timorese identified as such may vote and be eligible;
*The Assembly elects a Governor of the Territory;
*The Assembly and the Governor have a 5-year mandate;
*The Territory may enter into trade relations with foreign countries, promulgate its own laws affecting investment, land ownership, property, immigration, etc.;
*Remaining Indonesian troops are withdrawn within three months;
*The Territory will have no army. A police force is trained by the UN and is placed under the elected governor;
*Further reduction of Indonesian civil servants;
*Portugal and Indonesia normalise relations.

The second phase can be extended only if a 2/3 majority of the Assembly deputies vote for such an extension and this recommendation has to be put to a referendum.

This referendum is a safeguard for the people since there is no guarantee that the Territorial Assembly members will reflect the true sentiments of the people on such a crucial issue.

It is obvious that if the result of this referendum results in a majority rejection of the extension of the autonomy status the implication will be that the people will reject integration in Indonesia.

Phase Three (referendum on self-determination)
If the Territorial Assembly rejects an extension of the autonomy phase, or if the Assembly votes in support of an extension but this vote is rejected in a referendum, then the final status of the territory is resolved.
A UN-supervised referendum is held on the three options provided for in the UN GA Res. 1514 (XV) of 15 December 1960: independence, free association (with the colonial power Portugal) or integration with another independent state (Indonesia).
A referendum must be held within one year of the end of Phase Two.

ENDNOTES

1. Bertha von Suttner received the Nobel Peace Prize in 1905. For her relationship to Nobel see the article by Irwin Abrams, "Bertha von Suttner and Alfred Nobel," in Scanorama (Stockholm: November 1993): 52–56. Also on the website www.irwinabrams.com.
2. Fretilin was the abbreviation for the Revolutionary Front for an Independent East Timor.
3. Albert John Lutuli of South Africa was the president of the African National Congress.
4. The Wisdom of Sirach, also called Ecclesiasticus, is not included in the Hebrew Bible nor accepted by the Protestants, but it is extensively used by the Catholic Church in its liturgy. It is attributed to a Hebrew sage who lived in the second century B.C. The translation in *the Saint Joseph Edition of the New American Bible* (1970) is
    > "Peoples will speak of his wisdom,
    > and in assembly sing his praises
    > While he lives he is one out of a thousand,
    > and when he dies his renown will not cease."
5. More commonly translated into English as "I am a man: nothing human is alien to me."
6. The decree Gaudium et Spes ("Joy and Hope"), issued in the final session of Vatican II, deals with The Pastoral Constitution on the Church in the Modern World.
7. Wei Jing Sheng was a Chinese dissident, then in prison, released in 1997.
8. The actual words of Martin Luther King, Jr. in his last sermon, delivered in Memphis, Tennessee, on April 3, 1968, on the eve of his assassination, were "Like anybody, I would like to live a long life. Longevity has its place. But I'm not concerned about that now. I just want to do God's will. And He's allowed me to go up to the mountain. And I've looked over. And I've seen the promised land." "I See the Promised Land," in James M. Washington, ed., *A Testament of Hope: The Essential Writings and Speeches of Martin Luther King, Jr.* (San Francisco: Harper, 1991): 286.
9. Mairead Corrigan (later Mrs. Maguire) was a co-recipient of the 1976 Nobel Peace Prize in 1977.
10. Aung San Suu Kyi of Myanmar (Burma) was released from house arrest in 2002 but once again detained.
11. The Society of Salesians, named after St. Francis de Sales, was founded in Turin, Italy, by St. John Bosco (1815–1898). Its constitution emphasized the Christian education of the young, especially the poor.
12. These five principles included nationalism, internationalism (or humanitarianism), democracy, social justice and belief in God. They were part of the preamble of the very first constitution of the newly independent Indonesian state in 1945 and in subsequent constitutions.
13. The Nobel Peace Prize of 1994 was shared by Rabin, Shimon Peres, Foreign Minister of Israel, and Chairman Yasser Arafat of the Palestine Liberation Organisation, who became President of the Palestinian National Authority.
14. The decision for the peace awards is made by the Norwegian Nobel Committee alone. This committee is appointed by the Norwegian parliament, but it is not responsible for these decisions to either Norway's parliament or its government.
15. The French Cardinal Roger Etchegaray represented the Vatican at the award ceremony in Oslo on December 10, 1996. He was the head of the Pontifical Council for Justice and Peace and a friend of Bishop Belo.
16. In the original text this whole paragraph is printed as a quotation from Genesis. Actually the first two lines are the words of Bishop Belo himself. The

only relevant phrase from Genesis, 1.26, in the *Saint Joseph Edition of the New American Bible* is "Let us make man in our image, after our likeness."
17. Luís de Camões (1524–1580), Portuguese author of the epic poem, *The Lusiads*, the greatest figure in Portuguese literature; Fernando Pessoa (1888–1935), Portuguese poet; Agostinho Neto (1927–1979), the first president of independent Angola; Jorge Amado (1912–2001), popular Brazilian novelist; Xanana Gusmão (1946–). Leader of the East Timorese armed resistance to Indonesia, captured and imprisoned, but freed and elected first president of independent East Timor.
18. Later in this lecture Ramos-Horta greets representatives of the other lusophone (Portuguese-speaking) regions of the world.
19. Vicar General of Diocese of Dili, Belo's predecessor as apostolic administrator. Removed in 1983 because of his vocal opposition to the atrocities of the Indonesian army. In exile he worked tirelessly for the cause of East Timor until his death in Lisbon in 1991. The Foundation named after him has now been established and has begun training and research programs in conflict resolution.
20. In 1965 General Suharto led a military takeover of power, suppressed the Communists and then replaced Sukarno as president.
21. Most of the Jewish refugees on the ship *St. Louis* had visas to enter the United States, which were dated to be activated after a three-month wait in Cuba. The visas for Cuba, however, had been sold to them in Germany by swindlers and were invalid. The U.S. immigration officials refused to recognize the U.S. visas dated later, and the *St. Louis* had to take the refugees back across the Atlantic. Fortunately, European countries admitted most of them, but many had to return to Germany to an uncertain fate.
22. Indonesia did not have a valid claim to East Timor. The Dutch East Indies, which were transferred by The Netherlands to Indonesia under pressure from the United States, did not include the eastern half of the island of Timor, which had been colonised by Portugal in the 16th century. When Indonesia invaded East Timor in 1975 and later annexed it, the United Nations and most states continued to regard East Timor as a Portuguese colony.
23. Ramos-Horta refers to the Congress of Berlin of 1885, when the Great Powers made agreements regarding their African colonies. In the next fifteen years they divided up much of Africa among themselves.
24. After the Spanish colony of Western Sahara was annexed by Morocco, a nationalist movement, the Polisario, sought independence. UN efforts to hold a referendum kept being postponed by Morocco. In June 2004 former U.S. Secretary of State James A. Baker, UN Secretary General Kofi Annan's personal envoy to Western Sahara, resigned in frustration.
25. In 1988 Fretilin was reorganized into the National Council of Maubere (Timorese) Resistance (CNRM), of which Ramos-Horta became co-chair. In 1992 the CNRM Peace Plan was drafted and approved by Gusmão before he was captured in November of that year. This plan was proposed as the basis for a dialogue with Indonesia and presented by Ramos-Horta to international bodies such as the United Nations and the European Parliament., Still seeking dialogue with Indonesia in 1996, Ramos-Horta discussed the peace plan in his lecture and included it to be printed here.
26. ASEAN is the abbreviation of the Association of Southeast Asian Nations, APEC of Asia-Pacific Economic Cooperation.
27. Megawati Sukarnoputri, the daughter of President Sukarno, leader of the Democratic Party of Indonesia (PDI) became vice president, then president of Indonesia. She was a candidate to remain in office in the election of 2004, the result of which was not yet decided as of this writing.
28. SLORC, The State Law and Order Restoration Council, was the military government of Burma (Myanmar).

SELECTED BIBLIOGRAPHY

Primary Sources

Belo, Carlos Filipe Ximenes. "Nobel Lecture," in *Les Prix Nobel 1996* (Stockholm: Nobel Foundation, 1997): 319–326, the official publicaion.

Ramos-Horta, José. "From Kissinger to Albright: The U.S. and East Timor," *Pacifica Review* 12 (2000) 77–80.

——————— *Funu. The Unfinished Saga of East Timor*, 2nd printing. Lawrenceville, New Jersey: Red Sea Press, 1996. Preface by Noam Chomsky. A personal account of his efforts on behalf of East Timor through 1985.

———————. "Nobel Lecture," in *Les Prix Nobel 1996* (Stockholm Nobel Foundation, 1997): 330–344.

———————. "Taiwan and East Timor, Human Rights, Rule of Law, Self-Determination," *International Journal of Peace Studies* 4(1) (1999): 97–107.

Secondary Sources

Carey, Peter, ed. *East Timor at the Crossroads: The Forging of a Nation*. Honolulu: University of Hawaii Press, 1995.

Cobban, Helena. *The Moral Architecture of World Peace. Nobel Laureates Discuss Our Global Future*. Charlottesville and London: University of Virginia Press, 2000, pp. 80–95 and *passim*. Ramos-Horta was one of the laureates at this conference.

Hainsworth, Paul and Stephen McCloskey, eds. *The East Timor Question. The Struggle for Independence from Indonesia*. London: Tauris, 2001.

Kohen, Arnold. *From the Place of the Dead. The Epic Struggles of Bishop Belo of East Timor*. New York: St. Martin's Press, 1999. Introduction by the Dalai Lama. By a close friend of Belo, based on wide range of documents and interviews.

Marker, Jamsheed. An important memoir by the special representative of UN Secretary General Kofi Annan. He had much to do with this UN "success story."

Nines, Sarah, ed. *To Resist Is to Win. The Autobiography of Xanana Gusmão*. Melbourne: Aurora, 2000. Includes letters and speeches.

Suter, Keith, *East Timor, West Papua/Irian and Indonesia*. London: Minority Rights Group, 1997.

Peace 1997

INTERNATIONAL CAMPAIGN TO BAN LANDMINES

and

JODY WILLIAMS

for their work for the banning and clearing of anti-personnel mines

INTRODUCTION

In granting the prize to the International Campaign to Ban Landmines (ICBL), as Chairman Sejersted explained in his presentation address, the Committee was not only acting in accordance with Alfred Nobel's wishes about disarmament, but recognizing a new process of peacekeeping. Just as at the national level, where effective political action must be based on public opinion, internationally the ICBL, a collection of hundreds of non-governmental associations representing a worldwide grassroots public opinion, had cooperated in the so-called Ottawa Process with governmental and intergovernmental organizations such as the United Nations to form what was the beginning of a global civil society. The Committee's statement referred to this "as a model for similar processes in the future" which "could prove of decisive importance to the international effort for disarmament and peace."

For the award ceremony the ICBL chose the veteran de-miner Rae McGrath to give the Nobel lecture on its behalf and Tun Channareth of Cambodia, who had lost his legs to a landmine, to receive the tokens of the award. As Channareth moved his wheelchair to the podium to accept these, the audience rose to its feet in a thunderous ovation. His tragic story was told by McGrath, who also gave a moving anecdote about a little girl who was also a landmine victim. McGrath gave an eloquent speech, urging speedy ratification of the Ottawa Treaty by the states which had already signed and castigating the non-signers, telling them that they had "failed humanity" and were "intransigent and uncaring." The major powers not signing were the United States, Russia and China. President Clinton had originally spoken internationally against landmines, but the U.S. declared it needed landmines to protect its forces in South Korea but would not use anti-personnel landmines elsewhere and by 2006 an alternative for Korean defense would be developed. The Bush administration refused to accept such limitations on the use of landmines.

Jody Williams submitted a written text for the Nobel lecture but received permission to speak extemporaneously "from the heart". The written text provided a good brief history of the ICBL. Since the addresses of 1997, there has been further progress. The description of the ICBL on p. 59 takes developments up to July 2004.

ANNOUNCEMENT

The Norwegian Nobel Committee has decided to award the Nobel Peace Prize for 1997, in two equal parts, to the International Campaign to Ban Landmines (ICBL) and to the campaign's coordinator Jody Williams for their work for the banning and clearing of anti-personnel mines.

There are at present probably over one hundred million anti-personnel mines scattered over large areas on several continents. Such mines maim and kill indiscriminately and are a major threat to the civilian populations and to the social and economic development of the many countries affected.

The ICBL and Jody Williams started a process which in the space of a few years changed a ban on anti-personnel mines from a vision to a feasible reality. The Convention which will be signed in Ottawa in December this year is to a considerable extent a result of their important work.

There are already over 1,000 organizations, large and small, affiliated to the ICBL, making up a network through which it has been possible to express and mediate a broad wave of popular commitment in an unprecedented way. With the governments of several small and medium-sized countries taking the issue up and taking steps to deal with it, this work has grown into a convincing example of an effective policy of peace.

The Norwegian Nobel Committee wishes to express the hope that the Ottawa process will win even wider support. As a model for similar processes in the future, it could prove of decisive importance to the international effort for disarmament and peace.

PRESENTATION

Speech by Professor Francis Sejersted, Chairman of the Norwegian Nobel Committee, on the occasion of the award of the Nobel Peace Prize for 1997, Oslo, December 10, 1997.
Translation of the Norwegian text.

Your Majesties, Excellencies, Ladies and Gentlemen,

There are those among us who are unswerving in their faith that things can be done to make our world a better, safer, and more humane place, and who also, even when the tasks appear overwhelming, have the courage to tackle them. Such people deserve our admiration, and our gratitude. We are delighted and honoured to welcome some of them to the Oslo City Hall today. Our warm welcome to you, the representatives of the ICBL, the International Campaign to Ban Landmines, and to you, Jody Williams, the campaign's strongest single driving force. You have not only dared to tackle your task, but also proved that the impossible is possible. You have helped to rouse public opinion all over the world against the use of an arms technology that strikes quite randomly at the most innocent and most defenceless. And you have opened up the possibility that this wave of opinion can be channelled into political action.

We all know that the largest part of the task still lies ahead. Many nations, among them the largest, have been reluctant, at least so far, to commit themselves to not using this weapon. There is still the almost hopelessly huge and resource-consuming task of destroying the landmines — over one hundred million of them — that have been deployed. And the effort to build up opportunities for dignified lives for the many millions of innocent mine victims has only just begun. But through your self-sacrificing work, you have won support and created an organization that lead us to believe that it will be possible to reach the goal: a world completely free from anti-personnel mines. The course has been set, and the inspiration given. That is no small achievement, but a first step of very great and perhaps decisive importance. That step is what we honour you for today.

The mobilisation and focussing of broad popular involvement which we have witnessed bears promise that goes beyond the present issue. It appears to have established a pattern for how to realise political aims at the global level. The ICBL is an umbrella organization for over one thousand non-governmental organizations, large and small, which have taken up the cause. The Norwegian Nobel Committee wishes to honour them all, and to draw attention to the impact which such broad coordination can achieve.

A second characteristic feature of this process that ought to be noted is how, in the next instance, the political level was mobilised. A week ago, in Ottawa, 121 countries signed the total ban on anti-personnel mines. Through Foreign Minister Lloyd Axworthy, the Government of Canada took the decisive initiative in that mobilisation when, in October 1996, it invited all countries to the Ottawa meeting. "Such a treaty," Axworthy said in connection with the invitation, "can be a powerful force that establishes the moral norm — that the production, use, stockpiling and transfer of anti-personnel mines is to be banned forever." The strategy adopted, in other words, was not to water the treaty down with a lot of exceptions aimed at inducing the hesitant to join in, but to convey a clear message. Though this may have frightened some countries off, it has of course, because of the overwhelming support for the process, placed the larger nations under considerable political pressure.

The problem of landmines has been on the international agenda for a long time. It was discussed in 1980, in connection with the Landmine Protocol to the Conventional Weapons Convention. It was when negotiations on the revision of that Protocol were being held in 1995–96 that frustration at the lack of progress made itself felt.

In November 1991, the Vietnam Veterans of America Foundation in Washington, D.C. and medico international in Frankfurt agreed to launch a campaign aimed at banning anti-personnel mines. When the first International Conference on Landmines was held in London in May 1993, representatives of 40 voluntary organizations attended. The following year, in Geneva, 75 organizations were represented. Today, over one thousand organizations are members of the ICBL. It was by hooking into this popular involvement that the Ottawa process came to mark a new political beginning, lifting the cause out of the backwater it had drifted into.

It is interesting to watch this initiative apparently feeding back into the United Nations and the whole system of international negotiations, and giving them new life. Effective political action is dependent on cooperation at several levels. At the national level, that is old news, first given memorable expression over 150 years ago by de Tocqueville in his famous analysis of democracy in America. Representative political bodies cannot carry on politics in a vacuum. They need in some way or other to be rooted in public opinion. And public opinion must be formed and directed by the active involvement of individual members of society in society's manifold organizations or associations. These are the fundamental institutional elements of what we have learned to know as — a civil society.

The problem at the international level is that no global civil society has existed. Perhaps it is not so surprising that the UN has not always been able to be as effective as we might have wished. But in the extensive cooperation we have been registering between the multitude of nongovernmental organizations, the many national governments, and the international political system, first and foremost the UN, we may be seeing the outline of what may turn into a global civil society. We have glimpsed similar features in other connections, but hardly as clearly as in this particular case. In the bold hope this gives us for further development in the same direction, we see promising signs of a more peaceful world.

How did landmines come to be the problem that generated this kind of international concern? Weapons exist that in many ways are more terrible and pose a greater threat, nuclear weapons in particular. And is it not the case that by banning certain types of weapon, one indirectly legitimises the use of others, and thereby also legitimises war? What sort of peace policy is it just to ban certain types of weapon?

Certainly we have seen similar types of commitment, directed against nuclear weapons in particular, and the Norwegian Nobel Committee has on a number of occasions, most recently in 1995, called attention to active opposition to the build-up of nuclear arms.[1] There is a vast difference between nuclear weapons and landmines. The former are the weapons of the rich, the latter of the poor. Yet they also have something in common. Both hit victims at a vast remove from the actual warfare. They strike mainly at civilian populations, and their effects continue for generations after the end of the armed conflict. They are weapons which cast the shadow of war also across peace. War's threat to life and limb is everywhere and never-ending. To set limits to war's repercussions for civilian populations and its impact on times of peace has always been an important aim of genuine work for peace.

At this very time, while nuclear war casts its shadow over us all — and perhaps for that very reason has remained an unrealised threat since 1945 — landmines are exploding every single day. Nearly all those killed or maimed are the poorest and most defenceless among us, and probably number some 26,000 each year. Yet the most alarming aspect of the situation may not be that total itself, but the constant threat to the much larger numbers who live in the danger zones, who do not know where they can send their children out to play, or who can only gather fuel or work in the fields at great risk to their own lives. Such people have been robbed of the opportunity to use the land to build their own societies.

The ICBL and Jody Williams' work is work for disarmament. The Norwegian Nobel Committee has frequently honoured disarmament efforts, or work for the "reduction of standing armies," to use Nobel's own words.[2] Disarmament reduces tension and thereby the threat of war. The work of the ICBL and Jody Williams is, however, primarily aimed at what I have just mentioned: sheltering civilian populations from war. It is a humanitarian project. The Norwegian Nobel Committee's tradition of honouring humanitarian efforts goes right back to the first Peace Prize, awarded in 1901 to Henri Dunant, the founder of the Red Cross. Humanitarian work prevents war by seeking to eliminate the underlying causes of violence and war, the causes in the human mind. A humanitarian effort aims at "fraternity between nations," again to quote Nobel. It is a hand outstretched to the victims, both those who have been maimed and those in danger. It is a demonstration of care and compassion that transcends all national boundaries.

It is a paradox that what we find inside landmines is Nobel's brilliant invention, dynamite. Nobel was a profoundly moral man, and was deeply concerned about the potential of dynamite in weapons technology. At one time he developed a doctrine of deterrence. He wrote to his close friend, the peace activist Bertha von Suttner, that perhaps his factories were more effective in preventing war than her peace congresses. He cannot have been completely convinced, however. When he decided to establish a peace prize, the idea probably came from Bertha von Suttner, and it was not a fear-ridden peace he wished to honour, but a peace of reconciliation and brotherhood. The inspiration from Bertha von Suttner is reflected in the special mention given in his will to the organization of peace congresses as a criterion for the award. Bertha von Suttner was to become the first woman Laureate when she was awarded the Peace Prize herself in 1905, after Nobel's death. There have not been many women among the Laureates, and no doubt there should have been more. But let us at least take credit for having made an early start.[3] With her self-sacrificing, untiring and fruitful service to humanity and peace, Jody Williams is a worthy successor to Bertha von Suttner, who inspired the Peace Prize and brought Nobel to the realisation that peace must be rooted in the human mind.

An important step has been taken. The vast problem of landmines has effectively been placed on the international agenda. The worldwide opinion has been formed that something must be done about the problem. And the practical work of freeing the world from landmines has begun. It is in admiration, and in gratitude for their efforts to achieve that aim that we honour the ICBL and Jody Williams today with the Nobel Peace Prize for 1997. The vast and laborious task of putting an end to the production and sale of mines, destroying existing mines, and helping the victims has, however, only just begun. Let us therefore also express the hope that the process will win still greater support, so that the work can be intensified and a world without anti-personnel mines can become a reality in the foreseeable future.

International Campaign to Ban Landmines

THE INTERNATIONAL CAMPAIGN TO BAN LANDMINES (ICBL)*

The International Campaign to Ban Landmines (ICBL) was formally launched in 1992 by six non-governmental organizations (NGOs), Handicap International, Human Rights Watch, medico international, Mines Advisory Group, Physicians for Human Rights and Vietnam Veterans of America Foundation. It is a broad-based coalition of over 1,400 organizations in 90 countries worldwide.

ICBL organizational members include groups concerned with human rights, children, peace, disability, veterans, medical and other humanitarian needs, mine action, development, arms control, religion, the environment and women's rights. They work locally, nationally, regionally, and internationally to ban anti-personnel (AP) landmines. Since its inception, the ICBL has remained focused on its call for a ban on the use, production, transfer, and stockpiling of anti-personnel mines. Its goals include:

1. Universalization of the Mine Ban Treaty;
2. Compliance with the treaty provisions ;
3. Increased and sustained resource commitments for mine clearance, mine risk education and victim assistance, and for stockpile destruction;
4. Firm establishment of the norm, as an international standard of behavior by all.

A committee of thirteen member organizations and a staff of six coordinate the ICBL (as of July 2004). 1997 Nobel Peace Prize Co-Laureate Jody Williams and Mr. Tun Channareth, a landmine survivor from Cambodia, are the ICBL's appointed International Ambassadors, and serve as Campaign spokespersons. Song Kosal is the ICBL's Youth Ambassador.

Its working groups on Mine Action, Victim Assistance, the Treaty and Non-State Actors lead efforts to address all aspects of the global landmine crisis.

The work of the International Campaign to Ban Landmines has brought about tremendous change in a short period of time. In Ottawa, in December 1997, 122 countries signed a treaty that bans the use, production, stockpiling, and transfer of anti-personnel mines.

---

*The original description of the ICBL published in *Les Prix Nobel 1997* has been replaced by this new description of the organization as of July 2004, which has been kindly provided by the ICBL office. Minor editorial adjustments have been made.

To date over 143 countries have joined the Mine Ban Treaty and are full States Parties while another 9 have signed but yet to ratify. On 1 March 1999 the Mine Ban Treaty became binding international law faster than any other major international treaty in history.

To facilitate implementation of the Treaty, in June 1998 the ICBL developed *Landmine Monitor*, a unique civil society-based reporting network to collect information on and evaluate the overall progress of the international community in implementing the ban treaty, eradicating the weapon, and alleviating the landmine crisis. *Landmine Monitor* builds upon the expertise and capacities of non-governmental organizations (NGOs) and other elements of civil society to systematically monitor and document governmental compliance with Treaty obligations, as well as sustained progress in providing assistance to mine victims and mine action programs. The *Landmine Monitor* includes a global reporting network of some 110 researchers in 90 countries. The *Landmine Monitor Reports* are issued each year to coincide with the annual meetings of States Parties to the Mine Ban Treaty. This marks the first time that NGOs have come together in a sustained and coordinated way to monitor and report on the implementation of an international disarmament or humanitarian law treaty. Its reports are viewed internationally as the baseline from which to analyze implementation of and compliance with the Treaty, and have received widespread acclaim from governments, the media and NGOs alike.

There has been a great deal of progress in terms of implementation of the Mine Ban Treaty and the growth of an international norm against mine use, yet there are still many challenges ahead. ICBL continues to campaign, and strengthen civil society, worldwide. The ICBL plays an active role in the Mine Ban Treaty processes, including meaningful participation in Meetings of States Parties and the intersessional standing committees. ICBL activities currently focus on the following areas:

- encouraging full implementation of the Mine Ban Treaty. This includes monitoring of and lobbying for: destruction of stockpiled mines by the deadline within four years, clearance of mines within 10 years, delivery of effective victim rehabilitation and assistance programmes, submission of annual transparency reports by States Parties, and adoption of national implementation measures such as legislation;
- encouraging full universalization of the treaty (including urging signatories to ratify, governments that are not yet States Parties to join, and compliance by non-state actors);
- opposing mine use by anyone.

In 2001, the General Meeting, a biennial meeting of representatives of all national campaigns and organizations, approved the ICBL 2004 Action Plan, challenging itself to increased activity to accomplish as many of its goals as possible by 2004. 2004 is a critical year as the first Review Conference of the Mine Ban Treaty will be held in Nairobi, Kenya at the end of the year and that Review Conference will shape the next five years of work related to the Treaty and a mine-free world.

With the year 2004 approaching, in 2003 the ICBL undertook extensive and comprehensive consultations regarding the future of the campaign. In September of 2003, the General Meeting of the ICBL formally endorsed the concept of the ICBL reaffirming its original goals, and continuing to engage in the same types of activities as in the past, but in a gradually more decentralized fashion post-2004, with national campaigns, organizations and focal points playing an enhanced role where appropriate, and including a streamlined staff structure.

The ICBL has a calendar of campaign activities, which includes activities to mark significant anniversaries (1 March: treaty's entry into force, 3 December: treaty's signing, and 10 December, the annual Nobel Peace ceremony), actions targeting sub-regional and regional fora (such as the Association of Southeast Asian Nations and the African Union) and international fora (such as the Commonwealth) and action alerts responding to allegations of mine use or compliance issues. The ICBL also publishes several advocacy resources, including a Campaign Kit, available online in several languages, a Youth kit and youth website, and a quarterly "Landmine Update," available at http://www.icbl.org/update/landmines/. It also maintains a comprehensive website: http://www.icbl.org, where more information on the ICBL and its activities can be found.

NOBEL LECTURE

December 10, 1977

by

RAE McGRATH

Your Majesties, Members of the Norwegian Nobel Committee, Excellencies, Ladies and Gentlemen,

Almost exactly fifteen years ago somewhere close to the Thai-Cambodian border. Tun Channareth was lying helpless in a minefield, both legs shattered by an anti-personnel mine. As his terrified friend looked on he took an axe and attempted, in his own words, *"… to cut off the dead weight of my legs."* Horrified by the sight his companion snatched away the axe and dragged him from the minefield. Mercifully unconscious through loss of blood for most of the hours that followed he awoke to find his legs amputated. Today he lives with his wife and six children in Cambodia, he designs wheelchairs and works with disabled children, encouraging them to live full and active lives.[4] Tun Channareth is one of tens of thousands of campaigners from more than sixty countries who work in a worldwide partnership; the International Campaign to Ban Landmines (the ICBL). Reth was chosen to accept this prestigious award because he exemplifies the experience, commitment and activism which form the roots of this campaign, a coalition of more than 1100 nongovernmental organisations. We were, and still are, driven, not by the wish to ban a weapon of war, but to bring to a halt the unacceptable impact of the anti-personnel mines on people.

It is the indiscriminate nature of the anti-personnel landmine, the fact that it is triggered by its victim, that it remains active indefinitely after conflicts cease, which make it different from any other weapon. However, it was also its impact over such a wide area of human activity which singled it out — and made the birth of the ICBL inevitable. How could organisations committed to work with communities affected by landmines fail to recognise the fact which governments and the manufacturers had chosen to ignore — that the situation was already out of control and extending further beyond our capacity to respond with every new conflict? And armed with the facts about this weapon, how could civil society fail to respond?

Clearing landmines while others were being planted, manufactured and traded was no solution. Amputating limbs and providing prostheses for one survivor while another bled to death unaided was no solution. Why provide improved seeds for farmers whose fields were mined, or vaccinate animals which graze in minefields? We saw a world where peace had few advantages over war. The circle of manufacture, supply and use had to be broken. The answer was a ban — and so the campaign was born.

We called for a global ban on use, production, transfer and stockpiling and demanded adequate resources for demining and victim assistance. That call remains unchanged — a demand by civil society that governments throughout the world could not ignore.

In Ottawa last week more than 120 nations signed a treaty banning anti-personnel mines — a treaty which overcame the slow progress which had become the hallmark of international legislation. We applaud those governments who initiated and drove this process which began as a direct result of civil activism expressed through the work of the ICBL. The campaign, because of its diversity of experience and direct links to the minefields of the world, has been able to support the Ottawa process from the beginning; providing the humanitarian and technical data which underpins the urgent need to ban anti-personnel mines. We have praised the comprehensive nature of the treaty. But at the same time a key role of the campaign has been to identify and challenge areas of concern in the treaty since these could cost lives and deny land. For example; the treaty excludes "... *mines designed to be detonated by the presence, proximity or contact of a vehicle as opposed to a person, that are equipped with anti-handling devices...*" from definition as an anti-personnel mine.

Anti-handling devices are designed to kill or maim deminers. The Ottawa treaty rightly calls for signatories to assist and fund humanitarian mine clearance initiatives. It is, therefore, con-tradictory and against the spirit in which this treaty was conceived to include a specific exemption for a device which is designed to make that task more dangerous. Delegates at the Oslo conference which finalised the text of the treaty established for the diplomatic record that landmines equipped with devices which would explode as a result of an innocent or unintentional act were considered anti-personnel mines and therefore banned, the campaign will hold them accountable if this diplomatic understanding is not honoured. Allow me to put this in perspective.

Less than three weeks ago, on November 21st at ten-thirty in the morning, David Licumbi, an experienced humanitarian deminer, was working on the Lucusse Road in Moxico Province, Eastern Angola. David died when an antitank mine exploded less than a metre from him. He did nothing wrong, he broke no rules — a magnetic-influence anti-handling device fitted to the mine responded to the presence of David's mine detector. The implications of this incident go far beyond the tragic death of a deminer, work on this key road has ceased and this will threaten the resettlement of displaced Angolans and damage community confidence in the peace process. How can we ask these brave men and women to continue their work when their very detection devices may become the instrument of their deaths?

And so we view the Ottawa Treaty as a first and valuable step, a milestone in a battle to rid this world of anti-personnel mines. While these weapons remain in the world's armouries there is no nation immune from their effects — they can be delivered by aeroplane or missile and once they are deployed there is no magic technology to remove them — it would take no more than a few days to turn this country, Norway, into one of the world's worst-mined nations. It would take years to make it safe again and during those years Norwegians would become so familiar with the sight of limbless, blind and scarred compatriots that they would no longer turn their heads to look. Norwegians would become deminers of their own land and learn too late, as the people of Bosnia today are learning, that there is no immunity from the impact of this weapon.

To sign the Treaty is not enough, forty countries must ratify this treaty before its entry into force and no nation which seeks to reverse the damage done to our world by this weapon can justify any delay in ratification.

The International Campaign will do everything in its power in the coming months to achieve a legally binding ban by December 1998. To this end we, as Nobel Peace Prize Laureates — issue a challenge directly to the Heads of State of each signatory country — make sure that your country is among the first forty nations who ratify the Ottawa Treaty.[5]

What of those nations which have failed to sign the Treaty or those which have not even attended the preparatory conferences? It would be easy to focus totally on China, the United States and Russia, nations whose stubborn refusal to put humanitarian concern above ill-judged military policy is inconsistent with their status as UN Security Council members and major regional powers. But what of those countries like South and North Korea, India, Pakistan, Israel and Syria whose, often valid, concern for their border defences blinds them to the damaging nature of the anti-personnel mine? What of Egypt, a country which is itself blighted by landmines emplaced decades ago, which argues it needs anti-personnel mines to deter smugglers from crossing its borders? We have heard much about the South Korean minefields. South Korea and the US government argue that the Demilitarised Zone minefields are of such importance they wish to make them exempt from any landmine ban. The ICBL does not accept the defensive utility of and necessity for the retention of those minefields.

Freedom is so often the justification for war. But where is the sense in fighting for the freedom of a people employing a weapon which will deny those same people, in peacetime, freedom to live without fear, freedom to farm their land, freedom merely to walk in safety from place to place — deny them the freedom to let their children play without being torn apart by a landmine? That is no freedom.

All those States who have failed to sign this treaty have failed humanity-size, power and economy are irrelevant — they are intransigent and uncaring in the face of compelling humanitarian, economic and environmental evidence that anti-personnel mines should be banned.

We are determined that the Ottawa Treaty will become a global legal instrument applicable to all states and will leave no avenues of action unexplored to achieve that aim. Together we have achieved so much but our progress must be measured against an obscene reality — that there are warehouses overflowing with anti-personnel mines throughout the world. These weapons must be destroyed — their mere presence is a threat since, while they remain in store, any country which goes to war will be tempted to deploy them. The destruction of stockpiles removes that possibility.

The Campaign will focus particular attention on those nations which have not signed the Ottawa Treaty, especially those which manufacture, export or use anti-personnel mines. It is our contention that the treaty establishes a norm which is equally applicable to nonsignatories, that the use of anti-personnel mines by any force, from any nation including guerilla armies, is no longer acceptable.

And here we would offer another challenge to signatory states; illustrate your commitment by destroying stockpiles of anti-personnel mines and enact domestic legislation outlawing the design, manufacture, trading and use of this weapon immediately — do not wait for the treaty to enter into force, do it now.

Arms manufacturers have driven and encouraged the trade in landmines and profited from the misery of millions — we intend to hold governments to their treaty obligations which require them to stop all production of anti-personnel mines and their components. Who can forget the competition to ship millions of mines to Iran and Iraq, mainly from Italy, and the role of countries like Singapore in providing a "legal" conduit for those mines to reach their destination? Happily the Italian government has enacted legislation which has driven the worst offenders out of the business of landmine manufacture, a process initiated and supported by the ICBL — but our business with those companies is not concluded until we are assured that they have not merely transferred their production overseas. The supply of components implies no lesser culpability than primary manufacture. We should remember the lesson learned by the people of Sweden, who believed their country to have had no involvement in the export of landmines during the Iran–Iraq conflict. They were wrong — because the explosive which filled millions of Italian mines came from Sweden. And so we can be sure that today as a result of that trade cooperation, many years after hostilities between those two countries ended, a Kurdish farmer or a mother searching for firewood or a child playing in the snow will be killed or maimed by a mine like this (holds up landmine).

This is not an attempt to vilify selected nations — it is a plea for civil society to demand transparency from the arms industry, the military and from their governments. It is no moral excuse to wring your hands and cry "*but I never knew*" — if you never asked to know.

We have this target in view — that no soldier will carry an anti-personnel mine into battle. That no government or company anywhere in this world will make anti-personnel mines nor any weapon, by any name or in any shape, that is, in effect, an anti-personnel mine.

We will investigate all possibilities to achieve that target. Member organisations of the ICBL will continue examining the potential for mounting legal actions which may result in the payment of damages to mine victims, their families and mine-affected communities. Neither will we neglect the environmental impact of landmines. If a company can be held legally liable for an oil-spill we must ask why similar sanctions should not apply to arms manufacturers who have supplied landmines.

A small girl once explained patiently to me the moments following her crippling by a mine:

"We were playing a game by the railroad track on the hillside, we had to hop up the hill, we each took our turn. I was hopping and then there was a flash — a very bright light — and I thought there was a bang but my ears hurt and I could not tell. It was frightening and my friends ran away and I ran after them. But I fell over which made me more scared and I got up very quickly and then fell over ... and I slipped down the hill and I could hear my friends shouting and there was a strange smell and I started crying, I wanted my mother because I couldn't get up and run away or even sit up properly. Then I saw that something was wrong with my leg — it was twisted and very dirty and I saw it was bleeding — then I forget. When I woke up my face was wet, my mother was holding me very close and her tears were dropping on me. She said "Don't worry — you will be alright," I hurt a lot but I was happy then."

Anti-personnel mines do not only sever limbs, they can break the human spirit. We talk not of mine victims, but of survivors — but to survive such trauma requires support, encouragement and love. That responsibility must not be left to the survivors' family and friends, who are often struggling themselves against poverty and the damaging effects of conflict, but to a greater family — the human family. In most mine affected countries we, the international community, must offer more than the surgeon's knife and protheses as support to those who survive the blast of a landmine — in some countries even that basic level of care may not be available. This is not support — it is little more than first aid. In the same way as the Ottawa Treaty is only the first step towards a global ban, so prostheses should be seen as the first stage in the support process for the victim of a mine blast. That is not the case today, and the reason for this lack of response is evident and shames us all — we simply do not care enough. This is a responsibility which the ICBL places high on its action agenda. We must have respect for the rights of those who fall victim to landmines, most importantly their right to control their own lives and their right to be heard.

Through our member organisations, especially those who deal directly with landmine survivors and their families, we will seek effective and innovative ways to ensure support for their treatment to match the scale of the problem. That support must incorporate social and economic integration. The ICBL expects governments to join us in this attempt to redress the wrong suffered by the victims of mine explosions.

There are tens of millions of landmines around our world — no one knows how many and it simply does not matter. What matters is that we eradicate them. There is a popular myth that mine clearance costs too much — the ICBL does not accept that is true and, faced with the obscenity of the effects of the anti-personnel mines, it would be difficult to understand what scale of measurement could be used to make such a calculation. The problem is that most funding for mine clearance is allocated from aid and development budgets and, we would agree, those sources are inadequate to the task and are already struggling to meet their commitments in other sectors, often exacerbated by the peripheral impact of landmines especially in the fields of health, agriculture and resettlement. It follows, therefore, that other sources of funding must be identified. There should be no misunderstanding — the cost of global eradication of landmines will be billions of dollars, assuming that sustainable methodologies are employed and emphasis is placed on developing an indigenous capacity in each affected country.

We must afford it, we cannot talk of having concern for the global environment and yet leave future generations a blighted world with land made unusable by this deadly military garbage. We need to look for relevant funding sources which can meet the requirements of the task we face. It is worth making a comparison which illustrates the priorities which must be challenged before global mine eradication becomes an achievable objective.

The tens of millions of dollars spent annually on mine clearance pale in comparison to the hundreds of billions spent on the military. In 1995 alone the military expenditure by European Union nations was more than US$166 billion — in the same year world military expenditure was over US$695 billion. Based on these figures it would seem that the military, who are responsible for the laying of landmines, are polluters who can afford to pay the price of clearance.

But it is not merely a matter of making funds available, it is vital that they are expended on relevant, effective and integrated response. Mine action is a sector of development — that this approach works on a national level is well illustrated in Afghanistan.

To achieve these aims the campaign will continue to expand our activities and develop new national campaigns, particularly in countries which have not signed the treaty. We open our arms to new members who support our aims, particularly those from mined countries and from mine-producing states.

Your Majesties, Excellencies, Ladies and Gentlemen we are greatly honoured by the award of the Nobel Peace Prize and are proud but humbled to share this award with previous Laureates such as Nelson Mandela, Aung San Suu Kyi, Desmond Tutu, Bishop Belo and José Ramos Horta who have given so much in the service of peace. We would also like to take this opportunity to pay tribute to a fellow nominee and champion of civil action, Wei Jingsheng, and wish him well in the hope that he can one day return to his home in happier times.[6]

The International Campaign to Ban Landmines dedicates this award to all victims of landmines and their families, to those communities who struggle to exist surrounded by minefields and to humanitarian deminers. It is the wish of every reasonable human being to leave this world a better place for their having lived, it is a wish we rarely can hope to achieve. By eradicating landmines we can leave future generations a better and safer world in which to live — it is possible; we should grasp that opportunity.

Thank you.

The International Campaign to Ban Landmines was represented at the Nobel Peace Prize ceremony through its Steering Committee, comprising the following:

Afghan Campaign to Ban Landmines	Sayed Aqa
Cambodian Campaign to Ban Landmines	Sister Denise Coghlan
Handicap International	Phillippe Chabasse
Human Rights Watch	Steve Goose
Kenya Coalition of NGOs against Landmines	Mereso Agina
medico international	Thomas Gebauer
Mines Advisory Group	Lou McGrath
Physicians for Human Rights	Susannah Sirkin
Rädda Barnen, Sweden	Carl von Essen
South African Campaign to Ban Landmines	Noel Stott
Vietnam Veterans of America Foundation	Robert Muller

JODY WILLIAMS

Born 9 October 1950

Professional

As founding coordinator of the International Campaign to Ban Landmines (ICB), she oversaw the growth of the ICBL to more than 1300 NGOs in more than eighty-five countries. She served as the chief strategist and spokesperson for the campaign. Working in an unprecedented cooperative effort with governments, UN bodies and the International Committee of the Red Cross, the ICBL achieved its goal of an international treaty banning anti-personnel landmines during the diplomatic conference held in Oslo in September 1997.

In her capacity as ICBL coordinator, she wrote and spoke extensively on the problem of landmines and the movement to ban them. In recognition of her expertise on the issue, Ms. Williams was invited to serve as a technical adviser to the UN's Study on the Impact of Armed Conflict on Children, led by Ms. Graca Machel, former first lady of Mozambique.

Since February 1998, Williams has served as a Campaign Ambassador for the International Campaign to Ban Landmines (ICBL), speaking on its behalf all over the world, including at the United Nations, the European Parliament and the Organization of African Unity, as well in many national states. She is a member of the Coordination Committee of the Campaign, which carries out the strategies and action plans of the ICBL. She also serves as senior editor for its 1000-page annual Landmine Monitor Report, a groundbreaking system that monitors the implementation and compliance of the Mine Ban Treaty.

In the academic year 2003–2004 she also served as Distinguished Visiting Professor of Social Work in the Graduate School of Social Work at the University of Houston.

Jody Williams is one of 12 Nobel Peace Prize Laureates to work with PeaceJam, which describes itself as "an international education program built around leading Nobel Peace Laureates who work personally with youth to pass on the spirit, skills, and wisdom they embody. The goal of PeaceJam is to inspire a new generation of peacemakers who will transform their local communities, themselves, and the world."

Prior to beginning the ICBL, Ms. Williams worked for eleven years to build public awareness about U.S. policy toward Central America. From 1986 to 1992, she developed and directed humanitarian relief projects as the deputy director of the Los Angeles-based Medical Aid for El Salvador.

From 1984 to 1986, she was co-coordinator of the Nicaragua-Honduras Education Project, leading fact-finding delegations to the region. Previously, she taught English as a Second Language (ESL) in Mexico, the United Kingdom, and Washington, D.C.

Education

Ms. Williams has a Master's Degree in International Relations from the Johns Hopkins School of Advanced International Studies (Washington, D.C., 1984), a Master's Degree in Teaching Spanish and ESL from the School for International Training (Brattleboro, Vermont, 1976), and a Bachelor of Arts degree from the University of Vermont (Burlington, Vermont, 1972).

Honors

Awarded honorary doctorates from: Franklin Pierce College and Wesleyan University, 2003; the Royal Military College of Canada, 2002; Regis University, 2000; Shenshu University (Japan) and Rockhurst University, 1999; Williams College, 1998; Briar Cliff College, Marlboro College, and the University of Vermont, 1997.

Named in 2003 as one of "America's most innovative people over 50" by AARP *The Magazine*.

Received the Humanitarian Award, presented at the Hollywood Film Festival, Hollywood, California, October 2002.

Named Humanitarian of the Year, UN Association of the US, "Adopt-a-Minefield" Program, October 2002.

Named "Peacemaker of 1999," by the Oldender Foundation, Washington, D.C.

Awarded Clark University's Fiat Lux Award, which honors individuals "who have shown exceptional leadership in increasing humankind's understanding of issues crucial to the 21st Century," 1998.

Received from Nuclear Age Peace Foundation, Santa Barbara, California, "1998 Distinguished Peace Leadership Award."

Named 1997 Vermonter of the Year.

Named by *Ms. Magazine* as one of its 1997 Women of the Year; as one of *Glamour Magazine's* Ten Women of the Year; one of *Vanity Fair's* 1997 Hall of Fame and its 1998, "200 Most Influential Women in America series."

For further information about Jody Williams on the ICBL website, go to URL <http://www.icbl.org.amb/williams>, a page of background information about her, frequently asked questions (FAQ), articles and statements and latest updates. This page will also direct you to <long biography/CV>, with further information about her presentations, publications, speaking engagements, and participation in conferences and seminars.

NOBEL LECTURE

December 10, 1997

by

JODY WILLIAMS

Your Majesties, Honorable Members of the Norwegian Nobel Committee, Excellencies and Honored Guests,

It is a privilege to be here today, together with other repre-sentatives of the International Campaign to Ban Landmines, to receive jointly the 1997 Nobel Peace Prize. Our appreciation goes to those who nominated us and to the Nobel Committee for chosing this year to recognize, from among so many other nominees who have worked diligently for peace, the work of the International Campaign.

I am deeply honored — but whatever personal recognition derives from this award, I believe that this high tribute is the result of the truly historic achievement of this humanitarian effort to rid the world of one indiscriminate weapon. In the words of the Nobel Committee, the International Campaign "started a process which in the space of a few years changed a ban on anti-personnel mines from a vision to a feasible reality."

Further, the Committee noted that the Campaign has been able to "express and mediate a broad range of popular commitment in an unprecedented way. With the governments of several small and medium-sized countries taking the issue up ... this work has grown into a convincing example of an effective policy for peace."

The desire to ban landmines is not new. In the late 1970s, the International Committee of the Red Cross, along with a handful of non-governmental organizations (NGOs), pressed the world to look at weapons that were particularly injurious and/or indiscriminate. One of the weapons of special concern was landmines. People often ask why the focus on this one weapon. How is the landmine different from any other conventional weapon?

Landmines distinguish themselves because once they have been sown, once the soldier walks away from the weapon, the landmine cannot tell the difference between a soldier or a civilian — a woman, a child, a grandmother going out to collect firewood to make the family meal. The crux of the problem is that while the use of the weapon might be militarily justifiable during the day of the battle, or even the two weeks of the battle, or maybe even the two months of the battle, once peace is declared the landmine does not recognize that peace. The landmine is eternally prepared to take victims. In common parlance, it is the perfect soldier, the "eternal sentry." The war ends, the landmine goes on killing.

Since World War II most of the conflicts in the world have been internal conflicts. The weapon of choice in those wars has all too often been landmines — to such a degree that what we find today are tens of millions of landmines contaminating approximately 70 countries around the world. The overwhelming majority of those countries are found in the developing world, primarily in those countries that do not have the resources to clean up the mess, to care for the tens of thousands of landmine victims. The end result is an international community now faced with a global humanitarian crisis.

Let me take a moment to give a few examples of the degree of the epidemic. Today Cambodia has somewhere between four and six million landmines, which can be found in over 50 percent of its national territory. Afghanistan is littered with perhaps nine million landmines. The U.S. military has said that during the height of the Russian invasion and ensuing war in that country, up to 30 million mines were scattered throughout Afghanistan. In the few years of the fighting in the former Yugoslavia, some six million landmines were sown throughout various sections of the country — Angola nine million, Mozambique a million, Somalia a million — I could go on, but it gets tedious. Not only do we have to worry about the mines already in the ground, we must be concerned about those that are stockpiled and ready for use. Estimates range between one and two hundred million mines in stockpiles around the world.

When the ICRC pressed in the 1970s for the governments of the world to consider increased restrictions or elimination of particularly injurious or indiscriminate weapons, there was little support for a ban of landmines. The end result of several years of negotiations was the 1980 Convention on Conventional Weapons (CCW). What that treaty did was attempt to regulate the use of landmines. While the Convention tried to tell commanders in the field when it was okay to use the weapon and when it was not okay to use the weapon, it also allowed them to make decisions about the applicability of the law in the midst of battle. Unfortunately, in the heat of battle, the laws of war do not exactly come to mind. When you are trying to save your skin you use anything and everything at your disposal to do so.

Throughout these years the Cold War raged on, and internal conflicts that often were proxy wars of the Super Powers proliferated. Finally, with the collapse of the Soviet Bloc, people began to look at war and peace differently. Without the overarching threat of nuclear holocaust, people started to look at how wars had actually been fought during the Cold War. What they found was that in the internal conflicts fought during that time, the most insidious weapon of all was the anti-personnel landmine — and that it contaminated the globe in epidemic proportion.

As relative peace broke out with the end of the Cold War, the U.N. was able to go into these nations that had been torn by internal strife, and what they found when they got there were millions and millions of landmines which affected every aspect of peacekeeping, which affected every aspect of post-conflict reconstruction of those societies. You know, if you are in Phnom Penh in Cambodia, and you are setting up the peacekeeping operations, it might seem relatively easy. But when you want to send your troops out into the hinterlands where four or six million landmines are, it becomes a problem, because the main routes are mined. Part of the peace agreement was to bring the hundreds of thousands of refugees back into the country so that they could participate in the voting, in the new democracy being forged in Cambodia. Part of the plan to bring them back included giving each family enough land so that they could be self-sufficient, so they wouldn't be a drain on the country, so that they could contribute to reconstruction. What they found: So many landmines they couldn't give land to the families. What did they get? Fifty dollars and a year's supply of rice. That is the impact of landmines.

It was the NGOs, the non-governmental organizations, who began to seriously think about trying to deal with the root of the problem — to eliminate the problem, it would be necessary to eliminate the weapon. The work of NGOs across the board was affected by the landmines in the developing world. Children's groups, development organizations, refugee organizations, medical and humanitarian relief groups — all had to make huge adjustments in their programs to try to deal with the landmine crisis and its impact on the people they were trying to help. It was also in this period that the first NGO humanitarian demining organizations were born — to try to return contaminated land to rural communities.

It was a handful of NGOs, with their roots in humanitarian and human rights work, which began to come together, in late 1991 and early 1992, in an organized effort to ban anti-personnel landmines. In October of 1992, Handicap International, Human Rights Watch, Medico International, Mines Advisory Group, Physicians for Human Rights and Vietnam Veterans of America Foundation came together to issue a "Joint Call to Ban Anti-personnel Landmines." These organizations, which became the steering committee of the International Campaign to Ban Landmines called for an end to the use, production, trade and stockpiling of anti-personnel landmines. The call also pressed governments to increase resources for humanitarian mine clearance and for victim assistance.

From this inauspicious beginning, the International Campaign has become an unprecedented coalition of 1,000 organizations working together in 60 countries to achieve the common goal of a ban of anti-personnel landmines. And as the Campaign grew, the steering committee was expanded to represent the continuing growth and diversity of those who had come together in this global movement. We added the Afghan and Cambodian Campaigns and Rädda Barnen in 1996, and the South African Campaign and Kenya Coalition early this year as we continued to press toward our goal. And in six years we did it. In September of this year, 89 countries came together — here in Oslo — and finished the negotiations of a ban treaty based on a draft drawn up by Austria only at the beginning of this year. Just last week in Ottawa, Canada, 121 countries came together again to sign that ban treaty. And as a clear indication of the political will to bring this treaty into force as soon as possible, three countries ratified the treaty upon signature — Canada, Mauritius and Ireland.

In its first years, the International Campaign developed primarily in the North — in the countries which had been significant producers of anti-personnel landmines. The strategy was to press for national, regional and international measures to ban landmines. Part of this strategy was to get the governments of the world to review the CCW and in the review process — try to get them to ban the weapon through that convention. We did not succeed. But over the two and one-half years of the review process, with the pressure that we were able to generate — the heightened international attention to the issue — began to raise the stakes, so that different governments wanted to be seen as leaders on what the world was increasingly recognizing as a global humanitarian crisis.

The early lead had been taken in the United States, with the first legislated moratorium on exports in 1992. And while the author of that legislation, Senator Leahy, has continued to fight tirelessly to ban the weapon in the U.S., increasingly other nations far surpassed that early leadership. In March of 1995, Belgium became the first country to ban the use, production, trade and stockpiling domestically. Other countries followed suit: Austria, Norway, Sweden, and others. So even as the CCW review was ending in failure, increasingly governments were calling for a ban. What had once been called a utopian goal of NGOs was gaining in strength and momentum.

While we still had that momentum, in the waning months of the CCW review, we decided to try to get the individual governments which had taken action or had called for a ban to come together in a self-identifying bloc. There is, after all, strength in numbers. So during the final days of the CCW we invited them to a meeting and they actually came. A handful of governments agreed to sit down with us and talk about where the movement to ban landmines would go next. Historically, NGOs and governments have too often seen each other as adversaries, not colleagues, and we were shocked that they came. Seven or nine came to the first meeting, 14 to the second, and 17 to the third. By the time we had concluded the third meeting, with the conclusion of the Review Conference on May 3rd of 1996, the Canadian government had offered to host a governmental meeting in October of last year, in which pro-ban governments would come together and strategize about how to bring about a ban. The CCW review process had not produced the results we sought, so what do we do next?

From the third to the fifth of October we met in Ottawa. It was a very fascinating meeting. There were 50 governments there as full participants and 24 observers. The International Campaign was also participating in the conference. The primary objectives of the conference were to develop an Ottawa Declaration, which states would sign signalling their intention to ban landmines, and an "Agenda for Action," which outlined concrete steps on the road to a ban. We were all prepared for that, but few were prepared for the concluding comments by Lloyd Axworthy, the Foreign Minister of Canada. Foreign Minister Axworthy stood up and congratulated everybody for formulating the Ottawa Declaration and the Agenda for Action, which were clearly seen as giving teeth to the ban movement. But the Foreign Minister did not end with congratulations. He ended with a challenge. The Canadian government challenged the world to return to Canada in a year to sign an international treaty banning anti-personnel landmines.

Members of the International Campaign to Ban Landmines erupted into cheers. The silence of the governments in the room was deafening. Even the truly pro-ban states were horrified by the challenge. Canada had stepped outside of diplomatic process and procedure and put them between a rock and a hard place. They had said they were pro-ban. They had come to Ottawa to develop a road map to create a ban treaty and had signed a Declaration of intent. What could they do? They had to respond. It was really breath-taking. We stood up and cheered while the governments were moaning. But once they recovered from that initial shock, the governments that really wanted to see a ban treaty as soon as possible, rose to the challenge and negotiated a ban treaty in record time.

What has become known as the Ottawa Process began with the Axworthy Challenge. The treaty itself was based upon a ban treaty drafted by Austria and developed in a series of meetings in Vienna, in Bonn, in Brussels, which culminated in the three-week long treaty negotiating conference held in Oslo in September. The treaty negotiations were historic. They were historic for a number of reasons. For the first time, smaller and middle-sized powers had come together, to work in close cooperation with the non-governmental organizations of the International Campaign to Ban Landmines, to negotiate a treaty which would remove from the world's arsenals a weapon in widespread use. For the first time, smaller and middle-sized powers had not yielded ground to intense pressure from a superpower to weaken the treaty to accommodate the policies of that one country. Perhaps for the first time, negotiations ended with a treaty stronger than the draft on which the negotiations were based! The treaty had not been held hostage to rule by consensus, which would have inevitably resulted in a gutted treaty.

The Oslo negotiations gave the world a treaty banning anti-personnel landmines which is remarkably free of loopholes and exceptions. It is a treaty which bans the use, production, trade and stockpiling of anti-personnel landmines. It is a treaty which requires states to destroy their stockpiles within four years of its entering into force. It is a treaty which requires mine clearance within ten years. It calls upon states to increase assistance for mine clearance and for victim assistance. It is not a perfect treaty — the Campaign has concerns about the provision allowing for anti-handling devices on anti-vehicle mines; we are concerned about mines kept for training purposes; we would like to see the treaty directly apply to nonstate actors and we would like stronger language regarding victim assistance. But, given the close cooperation with governments which resulted in the treaty itself, we are certain that these issues can be addressed through the annual meetings and review conferences provided for in the treaty.

As I have already noted, last week in Ottawa, 121 countries signed the treaty. Three ratified it simultaneously — signalling the political will of the international community to bring this treaty into force as soon as possible. It is remarkable. Landmines, have been used since the U.S. Civil War, since the Crimean War, yet we are taking them out of arsenals of the world. It is amazing. It is historic. It proves that civil society and governments do not have to see themselves as adversaries. It demonstrates that small and middle powers can work together with civil society and address humanitarian concerns with breathtaking speed. It shows that such a partnership is a new kind of "superpower" in the post-Cold War world.

It is fair to say that the International Campaign to Ban Landmines made a difference. And the real prize is the treaty. What we are most proud of is the treaty. It would be foolish to say that we are not deeply honored by being awarded the Nobel Peace Prize. Of course, we are. But the receipt of the Nobel Peace Prize is recognition of the accomplishment of this Campaign. It is recognition of the fact that NGOs have worked in close cooperation with governments for the first time on an arms control issue, with the United Nations, with the International Committee of the Red Cross. Together, we have set a precedent. Together, we have changed history. The closing remarks of the French ambassador in Oslo to me were the best. She said, "This is historic not just because of the treaty. This is historic because, for the first time, the leaders of states have come together to answer the will of civil society."

For that, the International Campaign thanks them — for together we have given the world the possibility of one day living on a truly mine-free planet.

Thank you.

ENDNOTES

1. In 1995 the prize was awarded to Joseph Rotblat and the Pugwash Conferences on Science and World Affairs "for their efforts to diminish the part played by nuclear arms in international politics and in the longer run to eliminate such arms."
2. According to the terms of Alfred Nobel's will, the peace prize was to be awarded to the person who shall have done the most or the best work for fraternity between nations, for the abolition or reduction of standing armies and for the holding and promotion of peace congresses.
3. Jody Williams was the tenth woman peace laureate of a total of 87 individual laureates since 1901. In 2003 the prize was awarded to Shirin Ebadi of Iran, in 2004 to Wangari Maathai of Kenya, the eleventh and twelfth women Laureates of the total of 93 individuals.
4. Tun Channareth — Reth, as McGrath calls him — received the symbols of the ICBL prize at the award ceremony, representing the thousands of victims of landmines. Jody Williams, on the way to the podium to receive her own award, stopped before him in his wheelchair and solemnly bowed to him in the Buddhist manner in dramatic recognition of all these victims. As ICBL's "amputee ambassador," Channareth has traveled widely on behalf of the Campaign.
5. After the first 40 states had signed and ratified, the Ottawa Treaty came into force in March 1999. By 2004 the number of states ratifying had reached 143, and the ICBL and other supporters were hoping that by the first five-year review of the treaty in Nairobi, Kenya, in December of that year there might be 150 states which had ratified.
6. Wei Jinsheng was nominated when an imprisoned political dissident in China. In November 1997 he was freed to go to the United States for medical attention.

SELECTED BIBLIOGRAPHY

By Jody Williams

_____ and Shawn Roberts. *After the Guns Fall Silent: The Enduring Legacy of Landmines.* Washington, D.C.: Vietnam Veterans of America Foundations, 1995. The seminal study based on two years of field research in four mine-affected countries.

_____. Ethics and Politics: Comments to the 4th Summit of Nobel Peace Laureates, Rome, Italy, 27-30 November 2003. http://www.icbl.org/amb/williams/03_peace_prize_summit.html

_____. "Iraq and Preemptive Self-Defense," in *The Iraq War and Its Consequences*, edited by Irwin Abrams and Wang Gungwu (World Scientifc, 2003): pp. 17–48. A well-documented analysis.

Statement to Opening Session, 5th Meeting of States Party to Mine Ban Treaty, Bangkok, Thailand, 15 September 2003. http://www.icbl.org/news/2003/399.php

About Jody Williams

Cobban, Helena. "A New Model for Global Action: Jody Williams and the International Campaign to Ban Landmines," in *The Moral Architecture of World Peace. Nobel Laureates Discuss Our Global Future* (Charlottesville: University of Virginia Press, 2000) pp. 203–222. Jody Williams and Bobby Muller, ICBL co-founder, participated in this conference of Nobel peace laureates at the University of Virginia in November 1998. See also chapter 9 on Muller.

Current Biography, 1998.

"Jody Williams, ICBL Ambassador," http://www.icbl.org/amb/williams/

Other Sources

Cameron, Maxwell A., Robert J. Lawson, and Brian W. Tomlin, eds. *To Walk without Fear. The Global Movement to Ban Landmines.* Toronto, Oxford and New York: Oxford, University Press, 1998. Best introduction to the subject, with chapters by ICBL activists, diplomats, landmine victims and experts, scholars and others.

Maresca, Louis. *The Banning of Anti-Personnel Landmines: The Legal Contribution of the International Committee of the Red Cross.* Cambridge: Cambridge University Press, 2000.

McGrath. Rae. "Landmines. A Matter of Justice and Humanity," *International Journal of Human Rights* 2(1) (1998): 93–100.

_____. *Landmines and Unexploded Ordnance: A Resource Book.* London: Plato, 2000.

Mennesker Mot Makt og Mine. Oslo, Genesis Forlag, 1997. Comments by Norwegians, with English translations.

Rutherford, Kenneth. "The Evolving Arms Control Agenda: Implications of the Role of NGOs in Banning Anti-Personnel Landmines," *World Politics* 53(1) (2000): 74–114. By the co-founder of the Landmine Survivor's Network.

Winslow, Philip C. *Sowing the Dragon's Teeth. Landmines and the Global Legacy of War.* Boston: Beacon Press, 1997. Moving stories of human victims of landmines by a foreign correspondent who selects heavily mined Angola to illustrate the global problem.

Peace 1998

JOHN HUME

and

DAVID TRIMBLE

for their efforts to find a peaceful solution to the conflict in Northern Ireland

INTRODUCTION

In sharing the 1998 prize between John Hume, leader of the moderate Catholics, the Social Democratic and Labour Party, and David Trimble, leader of the moderate Protestants, the Ulster Unionist Party, the Norwegian Nobel Committee expressed its hope that the agreement they had reached on Good Friday in May of that year had laid the constitutional foundation for a lasting peace. The agreement replaced the direct rule of Britain by institutions of self-rule in the provincial Assembly of Northern Ireland and in its executive, Later that month the majority of the population of Northern Ireland approved the agreement in referenda, and in the autumn the newly composed Assembly with its government representing both sides met for the first time.

There were some, however, who thought that the peace process had not gone far enough, others, that the agreement had been premature. In his presentation speech Professor Francis Seyersted, Chairman of the Committee, declared, "We all know that major problems still lie ahead, and the new constitutional foundation for the peaceful resolution of conflicts is brittle." He thought that the peace process had produced a momentum, "although we must be prepared for minor setbacks as the process continues."

The more radical Catholic paramilitary Irish Republican Army (IRA) had declared a cease-fire, which remained in force, but an important provision of the Good Friday agreement called for the "decommissioning" or giving up of all "illegally-held arms in the possession of paramilitary groups," and those Protestants who were extremists claimed that the IRA would never faithfully carry out the terms of this provision. They said that Trimble never should have been sitting at the same table with Gerry Adams, who as head of the Sinn Féin (pronounced "shin fyne"), the political wing of the IRA, had participated in the negotiations for the agreement and had himself forsworn violence.

The Nobel Committtee announcement recognized the special contribution of each of the two prize winners. Hume had worked for years for the peace process, while Trimble had shown "great political courage" in leading the Protestant Unionists to the agreement. Sejersted called Hume "the architect behind the peace process and the solution chosen in the Good Friday Agreement," while Trimble, as "a relative newcomer to top-level politics … had the intellectual clarity" to know the time had come to be flexible and to compromise. Sejersted quoted former U.S. Senator George Mitchell, whom President Bill Clinton had sent to Northern Ireland for what was a successful mediation effort, "Without Mr. Hume, there would have been no peace process, without Mr. Trimble, no agreement."

The two gave very different Nobel lectures. Hume's was more personal, telling of the inspiration he had found in the evolution of the European Union, in the parliament of which he had been a delegate. He felt that "all conflict is about difference, whether the difference is race, religion or nationality," and he agreed with the "European visionaries," who "had decided that difference is not a threat, difference is natural," an "accident of birth." "Respect for diversity" was therefore "a most fundamental principle of peace."

Hume said the Good Friday Agreement gave the hope of "a future built on respect for diversity and for political difference." He wanted to see "Ireland as an example to men and women everywhere of what can be achieved by living for ideals, rather than fighting for them, to wage war on want and poverty ... where we build together a future that can be as great as our dreams allow." He closed with the words "We shall overcome," which he called "a quotation of total hope." He ascribed this to Martin Luther King Jr., "one of my great heroes of this century."

The heroes Trimble called upon in his own Nobel lecture were those he termed "the politicians of the possible." The best example of these whom he quoted often was Edmund Burke, an Irishman with a Protestant father and a Catholic mother. The others were Amos Oz, the Israeli writer, for reaching out to the Arab tradition, and George Kennan, the American diplomat responsible for the U.S. policy of containment of the Soviet Union.

Trimble explained that Burke challenged the doctrine that man was perfectible, asserting that humans are flawed and this is an imperfect world in which we must work. To him, fascism was "the pursuit of abstract perfection, the passion to change other peoples' personal, political, religious or economic views by political violence." He was thinking of the Communists and terrorists like the IRA. "A few fanatics," he called the IRA, "who dream of forcing the Ulster British people into a utopian Irish state, more ideologically Irish than its inhabitants actually want." To be fair, he also spoke of "fanatics who dream of permanently suppressing northern nationalists in a state more supposedly British than its inhabitants actually want."

All he asked for from the IRA paramilitaries was the beginning of disarmament, not on "precise dates, quantities and manner of decommissioning." He declared that the peace in Northern Ireland after the Good Friday Agreement was "still something of an armed peace. It may seem strange that we receive the reward of a race run while the race is still not quite finished."

Trimble's critics spoke of his lack of "the vision thing." He answered that vision means "clear sight. That does not mean that I have no dreams. I do. But I try to have them at night. By day I am satisfied if I can see the further limit of what is possible."

Unfortunately, the next election in Northern Ireland moved what would be possible further away. The extremists won on each side, the Sinn Féin received the majority of the Catholic vote, while the Protestant Democratic Unionists, led by Reverend Ian Paisley, outvoted Trimble's Ulster Unionists. This led to the suspension of self-rule in Northern Ireland and the return of direct government from London. Prime Ministers Tony Blair of Britain and Bertie Ahern of the Irish Republic worked hard to negotiate with the Northern Ireland parties but in vain. Decommissioning remained a problem, and the robbery of a bank apparently by members of the IRA was one more stumbling block.

In the elections of 5 May 2005 Trimble lost his seat in the British parliament, which he had held for fifteen years, while the two extremist parties, the Protestants of Paisley's Democratic Unionists and the Catholics of the Sinn Féin, headed by Gerry Adams, increased their majorities. Hume had already retired from politics due to ill health, and now Trimble, after his party's severe defeat, resigned as its leader. He claimed with some justice that the shift of Protestant opinion in favor of the Democratic Unionists had been the result of the failure of the IRA to disarm and to disband. Paisley pronounced the Good Friday Agreement as now "buried" and said that he would never talk with Sinn Féin.

In his Nobel speech, Chairman Sejersted of the Norwegian Nobel Commtttee had spoken of minor setbacks which the peace process in Northern Ireland might still expect. These elections seemed like a major setback to this process, but on 28 July 2005 the IRA declared that it was ending its armed campaign and would disarm and return to the Good Friday Agreement. The Democratic Unionists wanted to see IRA implementing its statement in action, but hope revived for the restoration of joint self-rule of Catholics and Protestants in North Ireland.

ANNOUNCEMENT

The Norwegian Nobel Committee has decided to award the Nobel Peace Prize for 1998 to John Hume and David Trimble for their efforts to find a peaceful solution to the conflict in Northern Ireland.

Over the past thirty years, the national, religious and social conflict in Northern Ireland has cost over 3,500 people their lives. John Hume has throughout been the clearest and most consistent of Northern Ireland's political leaders in his work for a peaceful solution. The foundations of the peace agreement signed on Good Friday 1998 reflect principles which he has stood for.

As the leader of the traditionally predominant party in Northern Ireland, David Trimble showed great political courage when, at a critical stage of the process, he advocated solutions which led to the peace agreement. As the head of the Northern Ireland government, he has taken the first steps towards building up the mutual confidence on which a lasting peace must be based.

The Norwegian Nobel Committee also wishes to emphasise the importance of the positive contributions to the peace process made by other Northern Irish leaders, and by the governments of Great Britain, Ireland, and the United States.

The Norwegian Nobel Committee expresses the hope that the foundations which have now been laid will not only lead to lasting peace in Northern Ireland, but also serve to inspire peaceful solutions to other religious, ethnic and national conflicts around the world.

PRESENTATION

Speech by Professor Francis Sejersted, Chairman of the Norwegian Nobel Committee, on the occasion of the award of the Nobel Peace Prize for 1998, Oslo, December 10, 1998.

Translation of the Norwegian text.

Your Majesties, Excellencies, Ladies and Gentlemen,

On Good Friday this year, an agreement was signed which has rightly been seen as a breakthrough in the efforts to achieve a peaceful solution to the long-lasting conflict in Northern Ireland. In the referendum on 25 May, the agreement won the support of a large majority of the people, and in June elections were held to the Northern Ireland Assembly according to the principles laid down in the agreement. This autumn, formerly irreconcilable enemies have attended the Assembly together.

We all know that major problems still lie ahead, and that the new constitutional foundation for the peaceful resolution of conflicts is brittle. This autumn, too, we have witnessed terrorist attacks in which several people have been killed. But it does seem as if these have been isolated occurrences, and that they have only served to strengthen the general demand for building on the foundations for peaceful solutions laid in the Good Friday agreement. The IRA cease-fire, an important condition for progress towards peace, remains in force. So, although we are aware that things can change rapidly in our unsettled world, the situation has been a different one since Good Friday of this year. The vicious circle of violence has been broken. The peace process has built up a momentum of its own which makes a return to earlier conditions of terror unlikely, although we must be prepared for minor setbacks as the process continues.

The Norwegian Nobel Committee has chosen two men who in its opinion should be specially honoured for their contributions to the peace process, John Hume and David Trimble. It is with great pleasure that we welcome you to our cold but peaceful north to receive the Nobel Peace Prize for 1998. You are foremost among the many who have placed themselves at the service of peace, in and outside Northern Ireland.

John Hume and David Trimble are both from Northern Ireland, where they have lived with and in the conflict. They are both prominent politicians, leaders, respectively, of the two largest political parties in Northern Ireland, parties which represent the two groups in a divided population. They have both committed themselves to the course which the Good Friday agreement represents: that conflicts must be solved by peaceful means. The strong support for the agreement in the referendum shows that they made the right choice.

Political leadership is not to trim your sail to every wind; it is to initiate movement, and to act at the right time. Like other political leaders, the two laureates have both helped to build confidence that it is possible to arrive at reasonable compromises by peaceful means. As political leaders, they are guarantors to their constituents that peaceful methods will lead to solutions which both sides can live with, and live better than if a state of war had continued. In a tense situation, such exposed positions require large amounts of both wisdom and courage. Today's laureates have shown both.

But there are differences between them. In 1970, at a time of spiralling violence, John Hume played a part in the foundation of the party of which he became the unquestioned leader, the Social Democratic and Labour Party (SDLP). It is a nationalist party, but it has stood firmly throughout for the principle that only peaceful means must be used. More than anyone else, Hume is the architect behind the peace process and the solution chosen in the Good Friday agreement. He has held unwaveringly to the line that discussions and institutional solutions have to be inclusive. Even those who had chosen violent means in their political struggle had to be given opportunities to participate in the peace process, to change their strategy, and to be taken at their word when they did so. Especially during periods of escalating violence, Hume has had to swallow sometimes very harsh criticism, from within his own ranks as well as from others, for his gentle approach to the hard-liners. But with his personal integrity, Hume has stood firm, and his policy has won through.

The Northern Irish Nobel Laureate in Literature, Seamus Heaney,[1] used the fable of the hedgehog and the fox to describe our two laureates and the difference between them. "John Hume is the hedgehog, who knew the big truth that justice had to prevail," he wrote. David Trimble, on the other hand, "is the fox, who has known many things, but who had the intellectual clarity and political courage to know that 1998 was the time to move unionism towards an accommodation with reasonable and honourable nationalist aspirations. In so doing, he opened the possibility of a desirable and credible future for all the citizens of Northern Ireland." When he was elected leader of Northern Ireland's traditionally largest party, the Ulster Unionist Party (UUP), Trimble was a relative newcomer to top-level politics. He was known as an uncompromising unionist, but soon showed that he had other political sides to him, and clearly felt that the situation demanded more flexible attitudes on the part of the unionists. Under his leadership, enough fear and suspicion was overcome to enable a majority of unionists to rally behind the Good Friday agreement. I need hardly add that Trimble, too, has come in for strong criticism for his conciliatory approach.

Only those who have themselves experienced having their rights trampled on, who have seen their loved ones killed, who have had to live with loss, fear and suspicion, only they can fully grasp what it means to live under such conditions or wholly understand the reactions such a situation provokes. In her book "A Strategy for Peace," the philosopher Sissela Bok, daughter of Peace Prize Laureate Alva Myrdal, writes about what she calls "The Pathology of Partisanship," about how war can create in us a mental state which leaves us devoid of respect, even of pity, for even the most innocent victims. She recalls the writer Stephen Spender's horror at finding that pathological condition in himself in the Spanish Civil War. Only through strong leadership and institutional guarantees can a society withstand such destructiveness, Sissela Bok concludes.

We who are looking on from the outside must be humble and slow to judge — judging is not our business. But the conflict does also involve us. It tells us something about ourselves by bringing general human features to light. The pathology of partisanship is one such feature. It tells us something about why violence engenders violence. It is remarkable, and promising, that despite such a cycle, despite the extremes in Northern Ireland, we are seeing more and more individuals standing up and proclaiming that forgiveness and reconciliation are more important than retaliation. Looking about us in the world, we see that people seeking peace following a violent past generally seem to find that the cry for justice must be subordinated to the call for reconciliation and amnesty. That is what we have learned for instance from South Africa.[2] And who, after all, are the just in a situation like the one in Northern Ireland, with two clashing views of reality? Meanwhile, we also learn, with Sissela Bok, how important strong leadership and institutional guarantees are in building up that desire for reconciliation which can move us away from a state of violence. Our laureates stand for such leadership.

I have already mentioned that they have both been criticised for their moderate and inclusive approach. There has been so much fear and suspicion that for many it has become difficult to believe in the other party's good intentions. The adoption of an inclusive strategy implies a deliberate break with suspicion, a disregard for fear. That, precisely, is the strategy of reconciliation. No doubt there are situations in which it is naïve to believe in the other party's good faith. To do so may be risky. But a real peace process needs people who are willing to take that risk. We need the bold — or, if you will, the credulous — people who are willing to stretch out a hand. It is surprising to see what a disarming effect innocence can sometimes have on the other party.

In addition to leadership, we need institutional guarantees, again according to Sissela Bok.[3] The Good Friday agreement provides institutional guarantees. It neither represents nor was intended to represent any agreement at the substantive level. Unionists are still unionists and nationalists are still nationalists. What they have acquired are institutions for the peaceful resolution of conflicts.

Permit me a brief parallel with our own experience. In 1814, Norway was forced into a union with Sweden. War broke out on Norwegian soil between the Norwegian peasant army and the professional Swedish army, which had returned from the continent after helping to defeat Napoleon. The fighting in Norway was brought to an end when the great powers intervened. They decided, Great Britain among them, that Norway must enter the union. But Norway was allowed to retain her new constitutional system. Armaments were replaced by political institutions. To reverse Clausewitz's famous aphorism, politics became the continuation of war by other means.[4] Ninety-one years later, the union was peacefully dissolved. The peaceful relation between the two parties was given symbolic expression when the Swede Alfred Nobel made the Norwegians responsible for awarding the Peace Prize.

In 1977, the Norwegian Nobel Committee awarded the Peace Prize for 1976 to Mairead Corrigan and Betty Williams, Northern Ireland's Peace People.[5] It has since been said that the time was not ripe. This time, too, we have heard that our choice may be premature, that lasting peace is still far to seek. The argument is easy to understand, and nothing could have pleased us more than to have been able to say today that peace was certain. But in connection with these awards, as with a number of others, the Committee bore in mind Nobel's clear intention that the Prize should reflect current affairs, and that it should advance the cause of peace. We know that a peace process may be long and difficult and suffer frequent reverses. In such processes, it is important to focus on the advances, made perhaps against the odds, and on the persons brave enough to stand up in a good cause. Reverses do not mean that their efforts have been in vain. They may have laid the foundations for renewed efforts at the next opportunity. That is how peace is built, slowly, like drilling through hard wood as Max Weber[6] put it. The work along the way is just as important as the finishing touch. And it is by drawing attention to the present stage that one may perhaps contribute to further progress.

Our two laureates have done great work in the cause of good. They have both shown great courage. So have many others: Gerry Adams, Bertie Ahern, Tony Blair and Bill Clinton, to name just a few of those who contributed most in the final stages of the process leading to the Good Friday agreement. United States' Senator George Mitchell, who made such a significant contribution as a mediator, gave an accurate description of the work of our two laureates, which I shall take the liberty of quoting: "Without Mr. Hume, there would have been no peace process, without Mr. Trimble, no agreement." It is a privilege for us to be able to honour you here today. At the same time, we know there are many difficult tasks ahead. We take comfort from the fact that you will still be heading the process, and that you enjoy good strong support from many sides.

JOHN HUME

John Hume is married to Pat and they have three daughters and two sons.

He was a leader of the non-violent Civil Rights Movement in 1968 to 1969 having established a record of community leadership through his founding role in Derry Credit Union, Derry Housing Association and his organisation of the "University for Derry" campaign. He was elected as an Independent to the Stormont Parliament in February 1969 for the Foyle Constituency. His manifesto committed him to forming a political party on the European social Democratic model. He did this with five other Stormont MPs and one Senator in August 1970. From its formation until 1979 he was the SDLP's Deputy Leader and has been Leader since 1979.

John's elective career has included membership of the Northern Ireland Assembly in 1973 to 1974, the Constitutional Convention in 1975, election to the European Parliament in 1979 (re-elected 1983, 1987, 1992, and 1997).

A key advocate of partnership, he played a major role in negotiating the Sunningdale Agreement. In the resulting Power-Sharing Executive of 1974, he served as Minister of Commerce.

In the period 1977 to 1979, John served as a Special Adviser to EC Commissioner Richard Burke.

As MEP he sits on the front Bench of the Socialist Group which is the largest group in the European Parliament. John has served on the Committee for Regional Planning and Regional Policy since 1979. He wrote the report on Regional Problems of Ireland (1987).

As Leader of the SDLP, he has led the Party in the New Ireland Forum Talks 1983, the Brooke Talks 1992, the Forum for Peace and Reconciliation 1994 and the recent All Party Talks which led to the Good Friday Agreement.

John Hume began talks with Gerry Adams with the stated objective of bringing an end to violence followed by All Party Talks, the objective of which was agreement that had to have the allegiance of both traditions.

John founded Derry-Boston Ventures and Boston-Ireland Ventures as part of the strategy to win new inward investment, marketing opportunities and trade/industry partnerships. He was co-leader of International Observer delegation — Filipino Presidential Elections (1995).

Awards
Irish "People of the Year" Award (1984);
American Federation of Teachers Human Rights Award (1986);

St. Thomas More Award, University of San Francisco (1991);
Irishman of the Year (1992). Awarded by "Irish Abroad";
International League for Human Rights Award for Peace and
   Human Rights (1994);
Order of Thomas More, University of St. Louis (1994);
Pio Manzu Medal, November 1994;
Communicators of the Year Award (RNID), July 1995;
European of the Year Award;
President Roosevelt Award, May 1996;
International Human Rights Award, 21 May 1996;
Global Citizens Award, January 1998;
Sean Mc Bride Peace Award, October 1998;
Nobel Peace Prize, 10 December 1998.

Honorary Doctorates
University of Massachusetts 1985;
Catholic University of America 1986;
St. Joseph's University, Philadelphia 1986;
Tusculum College, Tennessee Presbyterian University of America 1998;
Dublin City University 1994;
Boston College 1995;
Suffolk University 1995;
University of Nice, France, November 1995;
University of Notre Dame, Indiana 25 April 1996;
University of St. Andrew, 20 June 1996;
University of College Galway, 24 June 1996;
University of Santa Clara, June 1997;
University of Missouri, January 1998.

NOBEL LECTURE

December 10, 1998

by

JOHN HUME

Your Majesties, Members of the Norwegian Nobel Committee, Excellencies, Ladies and Gentlemen,

I would like to begin by expressing my deep appreciation and gratitude to the Nobel Committee for bestowing this honour on me today. I am sure that they share with me the knowledge that, most profoundly of all, we owe this peace to the ordinary people of Ireland, particularly those of the North who have lived and suffered the reality of our conflict. I think that David Trimble would agree with me that this Nobel Prize for Peace which names us both is in the deepest sense a powerful recognition from the wider world of the tremendous qualities of compassion and humanity of all the people we represent between us.

In the past 30 years of our conflict there have been many moments of deep depression and outright horror. Many people wondered whether the words of W.B. Yeats[7] might come true

> "Too long a sacrifice
> Can make a stone of the heart."

Endlessly our people gathered their strength to face another day and they never stopped encouraging their leaders to find the courage to resolve this situation so that our children could look to the future with a smile of hope. This is indeed *their* prize and I am convinced that they understand it in that sense and would take strong encouragement from today's significance and it will powerfully strengthen our peace process.

Today also we commemorate and the world commemorates the adoption 50 years ago of the Universal Declaration of Human Rights[8] and it is right and proper, that today is also a day that is associated internationally with the support of peace and work for peace because the basis of peace and stability, in any society, has to be the fullest respect for the human rights of all its people. It is right and proper that the European Convention of Human Rights is to be incorporated into the domestic law of our land as an element of the Good Friday Agreement.[9]

In my own work for peace, I was very strongly inspired by my European experience. I always tell this story, and I do so because it is so simple yet so profound and so applicable to conflict resolution anywhere in the world. On my first visit to Strasbourg in 1979 as a member of the European Parliament,[10] I went for a walk across the bridge from Strasbourg to Kehl. Strasbourg is in France. Kehl is in Germany. They are very close. I stopped in the middle of the bridge and I meditated. There is Germany. There is France. If I had stood on this bridge 30 years ago after the end of the Second World War when 25 million people lay dead across our continent for the second time in this century and if I had said: "Don't worry. In 30 years' time we will all be together in a new Europe, our conflicts and wars will be ended and we will be working together in our common interests," I would have been sent to a psychiatrist. But it has happened and it is now clear that European Union is the best example in the history of the world of conflict resolution and it is the duty of everyone, particularly those who live in areas of conflict to study how it was done and to apply its principles to their own conflict resolution.

All conflict is about difference, whether the difference is race, religion or nationality. The European visionaries decided that difference is not a threat, difference is natural. Difference is of the essence of humanity. Difference is an accident of birth and it should therefore never be the source of hatred or conflict. The answer to difference is to respect it. Therein lies a most fundamental principle of peace — respect for diversity.

The peoples of Europe then created institutions which respected their diversity — a Council of Ministers, the European Commission and the European Parliament — but allowed them to work together in their common and substantial economic interest. They spilt their sweat and not their blood and by doing so broke down the barriers of distrust of centuries and the new Europe has evolved and is still evolving, based on agreement and respect for difference.

That is precisely what we are now committed to doing in Northern Ireland. Our Agreement, which was overwhelmingly endorsed by the people, creates institutions which respect diversity but ensure that we work together in our common interest. Our Assembly is proportionately elected so that all sections of our people are represented. Any new administration or government will be proportionately elected by the members of the Assembly so that all sections will be working together. There will also be institutions between both parts of Ireland and between Britain and Ireland that will also respect diversity and work the common ground.[11]

Once these institutions are in place and we begin to work together in our very substantial common interests, the real healing process will begin and we will erode the distrust and prejudices of our past and our new society will evolve, based on agreement and respect for diversity. The identities of both sections of our people will be respected and there will be no victory for either side.

We have also had enormous solidarity and support from right across the world which has strengthened our peace process. We in Ireland appreciate this solidarity and support — from the United States, from the European Union, from friends around the world — more than we can say. The achievement of peace could not have been won without this goodwill and generosity of spirit. We should recall too on this formal occasion that our Springtime of peace and hope in Ireland owes an overwhelming debt to several others who devoted *their* passionate intensity and all of their skills to this enterprise: to the Prime Ministers, Tony Blair and Bertie Ahern, to the President of the United States of America, Bill Clinton and the European President, Jacques Delors and Jacques Santer and to the three men who so clearly facilitated the negotiation, Senator George Mitchell former Leader of the Senate of the United States of America, Harri Holkerri of Finland and General John de Chastelain of Canada. And, of course, to our outstanding Secretary of State, Mo Mowlam.[12]

We in Ireland appreciate this solidarity and support — from the United States; from the European Union, from friends around the world — more than we can say. The achievement of peace could not have been won without this good will and generosity of spirit. Two major political traditions — share the island of Ireland. We are destined by history to live side by side. Two representatives of these political traditions stand here today. We do so in shared fellowship and a shared determination to make Ireland, after the hardship and pain of many years, a true and enduring symbol of peace.

Too many lives have already been lost in Ireland in the pursuit of political goals. Bloodshed for political change prevents the only change that truly matters: in the human heart. We must now shape a future of change that will be truly radical and that will offer a focus for real unity of purpose: harnessing new forces of idealism and commitment for the benefit of Ireland and all its people.

Throughout my years in political life, I have seen extraordinary courage and fortitude by individual men and women, innocent victims of violence. Amid shattered lives, a quiet heroism has born silent rebuke to the evil that violence represents, to the carnage and waste of violence, to its ultimate futility.

I have seen a determination for peace become a shared bond that has brought together people of all political persuasions in Northern Ireland and throughout the island of Ireland.

I have seen the friendship of Irish and British people transcend, even in times of misunderstanding and tensions, all narrower political differences. We are two neighbouring islands whose destiny is to live in friendship and amity with each other. We are friends and the achievement of peace will further strengthen that friendship and, together, allow us to build on the countless ties that unite us in so many ways.

The Good Friday Agreement now opens a new future for all the people of Ireland. A future built on respect for diversity and for political difference. A future where all can rejoice in cherished aspirations and beliefs and where this can be a badge of honour, not a source of fear or division.

The Agreement represents an accommodation that diminishes the self-respect of no political tradition, no group, no individual. It allows all of us — in Northern Ireland and throughout the island of Ireland — to now come together and, jointly, to work together in shared endeavour for the good of all.

No-one is asked to yield their cherished convictions or beliefs. All of us are asked to respect the views and rights of others as equal of our own and, together, to forge a covenant of shared ideals based on commitment to the rights of all allied to a new generosity of purpose.

That is what a new, agreed Ireland will involve. That is what is demanded of each of us.

The people of Ireland, in both parts of the island, have joined together to passionately support peace. They have endorsed, by overwhelming numbers in the ballot box, the Good Friday Agreement. They have shown an absolute and unyielding determination that the achievement of peace must be set in granite and its possibilities grasped with resolute purpose.

It is now up to political leaders on all sides to move decisively to fulfil the mandate given by the Irish people: to safeguard and cherish peace by establishing agreed structures for peace that will forever remove the underlying causes of violence and division on our island.

There is now, in Ireland, a passionate sense of moving to new beginnings.

I salute all those who made this possible: the leaders and members of all the political parties who worked together to shape a new future and to reach agreement; the Republican and Loyalist movements who turned to a different path with foresight and courage; people in all parts of Ireland who have led the way for peace and who have made it possible.

And so, the challenge now is to grasp and shape history: to show that past grievances and injustices can give way to a new generosity of spirit and action.

I want to see Ireland — North and South — the wounds of violence healed, play its rightful role in a Europe that will, for all Irish people, be a shared bond of patriotism and new endeavour.

I want to see Ireland as an example to men and women everywhere of what can be achieved by living for ideals, rather than fighting for them, and by viewing each and every person as worthy of respect and honour.

I want to see an Ireland of partnership where we wage war on want and poverty, where we reach out to the marginalised and dispossessed, where we build together a future that can be as great as our dreams allow.

The Irish poet, Louis MacNeice[13] wrote words of affirmation and hope that seem to me to sum up the challenges now facing all of us — North and South, Unionist and Nationalist — in Ireland.

> "By a high star our course is set,
> Our end is life. Put out to sea."

That is the journey on which we in Ireland are now embarked.

Today, as I have said, the world also commemorates the adoption fifty years ago, of the Universal Declaration of Human Rights. To me there is a unique appropriateness, a sort of poetic fulfilment, in the coincidence that my fellow laureate and I, representing a community long divided by the forces of a terrible history, should jointly be honoured on this day. I humbly accept this honour on behalf of a people who, after many years of strife, have finally made a commitment to a better future in harmony together. Our commitment is grounded in the very language and the very principles of the Universal Declaration itself. No greater honour could have been done me or the people I speak here for on no more fitting day.

I will now end with a quotation of total hope, the words of a former laureate, one of my great heroes of this century, Martin Luther King, Jr.

We shall overcome.[14]

Thank you.

DAVID TRIMBLE

David Trimble was born in Bangor, Northern Ireland on 15 October 1944. He was educated at Bangor Grammar School, and graduated from Queen's University, Belfast in 1968 with a first-class honours degree in Law.

He was called to the Northern Ireland Bar in 1969, and, in the same year, became a lecturer in Law at Queen's University, Belfast. He was made Senior Lecturer in 1977, and, between 1981 and 1989, was Head of Department, Commercial and Property Law.

He married Daphne Elizabeth, née Orr, in 1978, and they have four children: Richard (22 March 1982), Victoria (5 April 1984), Nicholas (18 December 1986) and Sarah (2 April 1992).

He entered politics in 1975, representing (on behalf of the Vanguard Unionist Party) South Belfast in the Northern Ireland Convention, 1975–76.

Mr Trimble then joined the Ulster Unionist Party. He was Vice-Chairman of Lagan Valley Unionist Association in 1983–85, becoming Chairman in 1985. In 1990–1996, he was Honorary Secretary of the Ulster Unionist Council and, in 1989–95, Chairman of the UUP Legal Committee.

In 1990, he was elected MP at Westminster for Upper Bann Constituency, and still holds that seat today. He was elected Leader of the Ulster Unionist Party on 8 September 1995.

On 1 May 1997, the Ulster Unionist Party gained over 33 per cent of the vote in Northern Ireland, holding 10 of the 18 seats in Parliament.

Mr Trimble had been included in the UUP delegation in all-party talks in the early 1990s.

In 1996, he led the UUP negotiating team into another round of talks arranged by the United Kingdom and Irish governments. These eventually proved successful, the Belfast Agreement being concluded at Castle Buildings, Stormont on Friday, 10 April 1998.

On 22 May 1998, the Agreement was approved by 71 per cent in Northern Ireland (in a separate referendum in the Republic of Ireland, 94 per cent voted to remove the territorial claim from the Irish constitution).

On 25 June 1998, Mr Trimble was elected an Assembly Member for Upper Bann. The UUP, with 28 of the 108 seats, was the largest party. On 1 July 1998, he was elected First Minister (Designate) in the New Northern Ireland Assembly.

He was then charged, with the deputy First Minister (Designate), with implementing the Belfast Agreement. This involves creating an Executive Committee, responsible to the Assembly, though Mr Trimble and his party were insistent that the Irish Republican Army (IRA) would need to start decommissioning illegally held weapons before Sinn Féin is included in any such body.

Mr Trimble was also jointly charged with establishing a North-South Ministerial Council, linking both parts of Ireland, and a British-Irish Council, linking the two governments and other administrations in these islands. Mr Trimble was: Founder Chairman of the Ulster Society, 1985–1990; Chairman, Lisburn Ulster Club 1985–1996; Member of the Devolution Group, 1979–1984. He has succeeded in championing the Ulster Unionist cause internationally (helping establish a UUP office in Washington, DC in 1995); he was also President of the Unionist Information Office established in London in 1996.

His personal interests are classical music, opera, history and reading.

NOBEL LECTURE

December 10, 1998

by

DAVID TRIMBLE

The Nobel Prize for Peace normally goes to named persons. This year the persons named are John Hume and myself, two politicians from Northern Ireland.

But in one sense the singling of one or two persons, for a peace prize, must always seem something of an injustice. In Northern Ireland I could name scores of people, Unionist and Nationalist, who deserve this prize far more than I do.

Add to that the thousands of people who I do not know, but who have born witness, in their own lives, by carrying out what Wordsworth[15] called,

> "those little nameless, unremembered acts of
> kindness and love."

And since I know there are thousands of such heroes and heroines in Northern Ireland, how many more millions of peacemakers must there be in the front line of the fight for peace across the globe. People who stand in the front line for peace in all the places where there is no peace.

Naturally it is not possible to name each and everyone of those heroes and heroines who make up the huge host of peacemakers who, even as we speak, are at work for peace around the world.

But even if it is not possible to name them we can note their presence on the peacelines around the world.

Having said that, I am at the same time, anxious to allay any fears on your part that I might fail to pick up the medal or the cheque. The people of Northern Ireland are not a people to look a gift horse in the mouth. It is imperative that I take the medal home to Northern Ireland — if only to prove that I have been to Oslo.

And the way politics work in Northern Ireland — if John Hume has a medal, it is important that I have one too.

It is a truth universally understood that there is no such thing as a free lunch. That being so, John and I are obliged to sing for our supper. In short some expect us to speak as experts and hand out advice on how to make peace.

Some old hands say that there are two ways to sing for your supper. The first and the safest course, they say, is to make a series of vague and visionary statements.

Indeed are not vague and visionary statements much the same thing?

The tradition from which I come, but by which I am not confined, produced the first vernacular bible in the language of the common people, and contributed much to the scientific language of the enlightenment. It puts a great price on the precise use of words, and uses them with circumspection, so much so that our passion for precision is often confused with an indifference to idealism.

Not so. But I am personally and perhaps culturally conditioned to be sceptical of speeches which are full of sound and fury, idealistic in intention, but impossible of implementation; and I resist the kind of rhetoric which substitutes vapour for vision.

Instinctively, I identify with the person who said that when he heard a politician talk of his vision, he recommended him to consult an optician!

But, if you want to hear of a possible Northern Ireland, not a Utopia, but a normal and decent society, flawed as human beings are flawed, but fair as human beings are fair, then I hope not to disappoint you.

The second suggestion is that either John or I, or indeed both of us, might explicate at some little length, like peace scientists so to speak, on any lessons learnt in the little laboratory of Northern Ireland as if we were scientists and the people were so much mice.

Speaking for myself, there are two good reasons to reject this course. *First,* I am not sure that I hold the status of scientist in the political laboratory of Northern Ireland. Indeed, there have been days, particularly recently, when I have felt much less like the scientist and very much more like the mouse!

Secondly, I have, in fact, some fairly serious reservations about the merits of using any conflict, not least Northern Ireland as a model for the study, never mind the solution, of other conflicts.

In fact if anything, the opposite is true.

Let me spell this out.

I believe that a sense of the unique, specific and concrete circumstances of any situation is the first indispensable step to solving the problems posed by that situation.

Now, I wish I could say that insight was my own. But that insight into the central role of concrete and specific circumstance is the bedrock of the political thought of a man who is universally recognised as one of the most eminent philosophers of practical politics.

I refer, of course to the eminent eighteenth century Irish political philosopher, and brilliant British parliamentarian, Edmund Burke.[16]

He was the most powerful and prophetic political intellect of that century. He anticipated and welcomed the American revolution. He anticipated the dark side of the French revolution. He delved deep into the roots of that political violence, based on the false notion of the perfectibility of man, which has plagued us since the French revolution. He is claimed by both conservatives and liberals. He can be claimed by Britain and Ireland, by catholic and protestant, and indeed by the world.

For Burke's belief in the role of law and in parliamentary democracy, is not our monopoly, but the birthright of men and women of all countries, all colours and all creeds.

But of course he has special significance for us in Ireland. Burke, the son of a protestant father and a catholic mother, was a man who in word and in deed honoured both religious traditions, recognised and respected his Irish roots and the British Parliamentary system which nursed him to the full flowering of his genius.

Today as we seek to decommission not only arms and ammunition, but also hearts and minds, Burke provides us not only with a powerful role model of the pluralist Irishman, but also with a powerful role model for politicians everywhere.

Burke is the best model for what might be called politicians of the possible. Politicians who seek to make a working peace, not in some perfect world, that never was, but in this, the flawed world, which is our only workshop.

Because he is the philosopher of practical politics, not of visionary vapours, because his beliefs correspond to empirical experience, he may be a good general guide to the practical politics of peacemaking.

I shall also be calling on two other philosophers, Amos Oz, the distinguished Israeli writer who has reached out to the Arab tradition, and George Kennan,[17] the former US Ambassador to the Soviet Union, who laid the cornerstone of postwar US foreign policy.

All three, Burke, Oz and Kennan, are particularly acute about the problems of dealing with revolutionary violence — that political, religious and racial terrorism that comes from the pursuit of what Burke called abstract virtue, the urge to make men perfect against their will.

Now these negative notes do not mean I have not good news at the end. I do. But, it would be a dereliction of duty if I only conjured up good and generous ghosts, and failed to specify the spectres at the feast.

There are fascist forces in this world. The first step to their defeat is to define them. Let me now, with the help of Burke, Oz and Keenan, locate the dark foundation of fascism from which flows most of the political, religious and racial violence which pollutes the progressive achievements of humanity.

Burke believed that the source of the pollution is the Platonic pursuit of abstract perfection, the passion to change other peoples' personal, political, religious or economic views by political violence.

I say Platonic because that savage pursuit of abstract perfection starts in the Western World with Plato's Republic. It rises to a plateau with the French and Russian revolutions. It descended to new depths with the Nazis and is present in all the national, ethnic and religious conflicts current after the collapse of communism, itself the most determined and ruthless Platonic experiment in perfecting the economic system whatever the cost in human life.[18]

Burke challenged the Platonic perfectibility doctrine whose principal protagonist was Rousseau. Rousseau regarded man as perfect and society as corrupt. Burke believed man was flawed and that society was redemptive. The Revolution tested these theories and it was Burke's that proved the most progressive in terms of practical politics.

He had a horror of abstract notions. In 1781 he said,

> "Abstract liberty, like other mere abstractions, is not to be found."

Seven years later he opposed the revolution correctly predicting that the mob would be replaced by a cabal, and the cabal by a dictator.

At the end of Rousseau's road, Burke predicted, we would find not the perfectibility of man but the gibbet and the guillotine. And so it proved.

And so it proved when Stalin set out to perfect the new Soviet man. So it proved with Mao in China and Pol Pot in Cambodia. So it will prove in every conflict when perfection is sought at the point of a gun.

Amos Oz has also arrived at the same conclusion. Recently in a radio programme he was asked to define a political fanatic. He did so as follows,

> "A political fanatic" he said, "is someone who is more interested in you than in himself."

At first that might make him seem to be an altruist, but look closer and you will see the terrorist.

A political fanatic is not someone who wants to perfect himself. No, he wants to perfect you. He wants to perfect you personally, to perfect you politically, to perfect you religiously, or racially, or geographically.

He wants you to change your mind, your government, your borders. He may not be able to change your race, so he will eliminate you from the perfect equation in his mind by eliminating you from the earth.

> "The Jacobins," said Burke, "had little time for the imperfect."[19]

We in Northern Ireland are not free from taint.

We have a few fanatics who dream of forcing the Ulster British people into a Utopian Irish state, more ideologically Irish than its own inhabitants actually want. We also have fanatics who dream of permanently suppressing northern nationalists in a state more supposedly British than its inhabitants actually want.

But a few fanatics are not a fundamental problem. No, the problem arises if political fanatics bury themselves within a morally legitimate political movement. Then there is a double danger. The first is that we might dismiss legitimate claims for reform because of the barbarism of terrorist groups bent on revolution.

In that situation experience would suggest that the best way forward is for democrats to carry out what the Irish writer, Eoghan Harris[20] calls acts of good authority. That is acts addressed to their own side.

Thus each reformist group has a moral obligation to deal with its own fanatics. The Serbian democrats must take on the Serbian fascists. The PLO must take on Hammas.[21] In Northern Ireland, constitutional nationalists must take on Republican dissident terrorists and constitutional Unionists must confront protestant terrorists.

There is a second danger. Sometimes in our search for a solution, we go into denial about the darker side of the fanatic, the darker side of human nature. Not all may agree, but we cannot ignore the existence of evil. Particularly that form of political evil that wants to perfect a person, a border at any cost.

It has many faces. Some of these faces look suspiciously like the leaders of the Serbian forces wanted for massacres such as that at Srebenice, some like those wielding absolute power in Baghdad, some like those wanted for the Omagh bombing.[22]

It worries me that there is an appeasing strand in Western politics. Sometimes it is a hope that things are not as bad as all that. Sometimes it is a hope that people can be weaned away from terror.

What we need is George Kennan's hardheaded advice to the State Department in the 1960s for dealing with the State terrorists of his time, based on his years in Moscow,

> "Don't act chummy with them; don't assume a
> community of aims with them which does not really
> exist; don't make fatuous gestures of goodwill."

Let me commend those clear words to those who sometimes seem to think that dealing with fascists is merely a game where one won't get hurt.

My philosophers are also guides as to how best to battle against these dark forces. Here we come again to Burke's belief that politics proceeds not by some abstract notions or by simple appeal to the past, but by close attention to the concrete detail and circumstance of the current specific situation.

> "Circumstances give in reality to every political principle, its distinguishing colour, and discriminating effect. The circumstances are what render every civil and political scheme beneficial or noxious to mankind."

That is the nub of the matter. True, I am sure of other conflicts. Previous precedents must not blind negotiators to the current circumstances. This first step away from abstraction and towards reality, should be followed by the creation of space for movement.

This is what I have tried to do: to tell Unionists to give things a chance to develop. Given that the Ulster British people are coming out the experience of 25 years of "armed struggle" directed against them. They have given our appeals a generous hearing.

Critics say that concessions are a sign of weakness. Burke, however says,

> "Magnanimity in politics is not seldom the truest wisdom; and a great empire and little minds go ill together."

Prophetic words when we think of the history of the British Empire. And we Unionists are the inheritors of its intellectual and cultural traditions.

But the realisation of peace needs more than magnanimity. It requires a certain political prudence, and a willingness at times not to be too precise or pedantic. Burke says,

> "It is the nature of greatness not to be exact."

Amos Oz agrees,

> "Inconsistency is the basis of coexistence. The heroes of tragedy driven by consistency and by righteousness, destroy each other. He who seeks total supreme justice seeks death."

In Ulster, what I have looked for is a peace within the realms of the possible. We could only have started from where we actually were, not from where we would have liked to be.

And we have started. And we will go on. And we will go on all the better if we walk, rather than run. If we put aside fantasy and accept the flawed nature of human enterprises. Sometimes we will stumble, maybe even go back a bit. But this need not matter if in the spirit of an old Irish proverb we say to ourselves,

"Tomorrow is another day."

In not seeking perfection beyond the power of flawed man we are acting not just within the Burkean tradition but within the broad religious consensus. This is not a pessimistic approach: but a positiveness founded on reality.

Because politics is not an exact science, but partakes of human nature within the contingent circumstances of the moment, I have not pressed the paramilitaries on the details of decommissioning. Although I am under pressure from my own political community I have not insisted on precise dates quantities and manner of decommissioning.

All I have asked for is a credible beginning. All I have asked for is that they say that the "war" is over. And that is proved by such a beginning. That is not too much to ask for. Nor is it too much to ask that the reformist party of nationalism, the SDLP, support me in this.

But common sense dictates that I cannot for ever convince society that real peace is at hand if there is not a beginning to the decommissioning of weapons as earnest as the decommissioning of hearts that must follow. Any further delay will reinforce dark doubts about whether Sinn Féin are drinking from the clear stream of democracy, or is still drinking from the dark stream of fascism. It cannot for ever face both ways.

Plenty of space has been given to the paramilitaries. Now, winter is here, and there is still no sign of spring.

Like John Bunyan's Pilgrim, we politicians have been through the Slough of Despond. We have seen Doubting Castle, the owner whereof was Giant Despair. I can recall many passages through the Valley of Humiliation. And all too often we have encountered, not only on the other side, but on our own side too, "the man who could look no way but downwards, with a muckrake in his hand."[23]

Nevertheless, like one of Beckett's[24] characters, "I will go on, because I must go on."

What we democratic politicians want in Northern Ireland is not some Utopian society but a normal society. The best way to secure that normalcy is the tried and trusted method of parliamentary democracy.

So the Northern Ireland Assembly is the primary institutional instrument for the development of a normal society in Northern Ireland.

Like any parliament it needs to be more than a cockpit for competing victimisations. Burke said it best,

> Parliament is not a congress of ambassadors
> from different and hostile interests; which
> interests each must maintain, as an agent and
> an advocate, against other agents and advocates;
> but Parliament is a deliberative assembly of

> one nation, with one interest, that of the whole;
> where not local purposes, nor local prejudices
> ought to guide, but the general good, resulting
> from the general reason of the whole.

Some critics complain of a lack of "the vision thing."

But vision in its pure meaning is clear sight. That does not mean I have no dreams. I do. But I try to have them at night. By day I am satisfied if I can see the furthest limit of what is possible.

Politics can be likened to driving at night over unfamiliar hills and mountains. Close attention must be paid to what the beam can reach and the next bend.

Driving by day, as I believe we are now doing, we should drive steadily, not recklessly, studying the countryside ahead, with judicious glances in the mirror.

We should be encouraged by having come so far, and face into the next hill, rather than the mountain beyond. It is not that the mountain is not in my mind, but the hill has to be climbed first.

There are Hills in Northern Ireland and there are Mountains. The Hills are decommissioning and policing. But the Mountain, if we could but see it clearly, is not in front of us but behind us, in history.

The dark shadow we seem to see in the distance is not really a mountain ahead, but the shadow of the mountain behind — a shadow from the past thrown forward into our future. It is a dark sludge of historical sectarianism. We can leave it behind us if we wish.

But both communities must leave it behind, because both created it. Each thought it had good reason to fear the other. As Namier says, the irrational is not necessarily unreasonable.[25]

Ulster Unionists, fearful of being isolated on the island, built a solid house, but it was a cold house for catholics. And northern nationalists, although they had a roof over their heads, seemed to us as if they meant to burn the house down.

None of us are entirely innocent. *But thanks* to our strong sense of civil society, *thanks* to our religious recognition that none of us are perfect, *thanks to* the thousands of people from both sides who made countless acts of good authority, *thanks* to a tradition of parliamentary democracy which meant that paramilitarism never displaced politics, *thanks* to all these specific, concrete circumstances we, thank God, stopped short of that abyss that engulfed Bosnia, Kosovo, Somalia and Rwanda.[26]

Thank you for this Prize for Peace. We have peace today in Northern Ireland. But it is still something of an armed peace. It may seem strange that we receive the reward of a race run while the race is still not quite finished. But the paramilitaries are finished. But politics is not finished.

It is the bedrock to which all societies return. Because we are the only agents of change who accept man as he is and not as someone else wants him to be. The work we do may be grubby and without glamour. But it has one saving grace. It is grounded on reality and reason. What is the nature of that reason? Let Burke answer,

> "Political reason is a computing principle:
> adding, subtracting, multiplying and dividing,
> morally — and not metaphysically or mathematically
> — true moral denominations."

There are two traditions in Northern Ireland. There are two main religious denominations. But there is only one true moral denomination. And it wants peace.

I am happy and honoured to accept this Prize on my own behalf.

I am happy and honoured to accept this Prize on behalf of all the people of Northern Ireland.

I am happy and honoured to accept the Prize on behalf of all the peacemakers from throughout the British Isles and farther afield who made the Belfast Agreement that Good Friday at Stormont.

That agreement showed that the people of Northern Ireland are no petty people.

They did good work that day.

And tomorrow is now another day.

Thank you.

ENDNOTES

1. Seamus Heaney of the Republic of Ireland won the Nobel Literature prize in 1995.
2. For the Peace Prize of 1993 received by Nelson Mandela and President F.W. de Klerk of South Africa, see Irwin Abrams, *The Nobel Peace Prize*, pp. 297–301.
3. In her book *A Strategy of Peace: Human Values and the Threat of War* (New York: Pantheon, 1989), Sissela Bok refers to the experience of Sir Stephen Spender (1909–1995), English poet and critic, who fought in the Spanish Civil War. Bok's mother, Alva Myrdal of Sweden (1902–1986), shared the Peace Prize of 1992.
4. Karl von Clausewitz (1780–1831) was a Prussian general who wrote on military strategy. His famous dictum was that war was the continuation of policy (not of politics, as Hume said), by other means.
5. See Abrams, *The Nobel Peace Prize*, pp. 232–235.
6. Max Weber ((1864–1920) was a prominent German sociologist and economist.
7. William Butler Yeats (1865–1939) was the Irish poet, playwright and essayist.
8. The Universal Declaration of Human Rights was adopted by the General Assembly of the UN on December 10, 1948, fifty years to the day before Hume's lecture.
9. The European Convention for the Protection of Human Rights was drawn up by the Council of Europe of the European Union and adopted in 1954. The European Court of Human Rights was established in 1959.
10. The European Parliament is part of the European Union, which is an integrated body of 25 democratic states which have pooled parts of their sovereignty. Other institutions are the Council of Ministers, the European Commission and the European Court of Justice. The members of the European Parliament are elected within the member states, as Hume was. The Council of Ministers is composed of the foreign ministers of the member states. The European Commission is staffed by civil servants and may submit proposals of policy to the Council of Ministers.
11. The Good Friday Agreement provided for a North-South Ministerial Council, with ministers from the Irish Republic and Northern Ireland and a British-Irish intergovernmental Council.
12. The negotiations were internationalized. The prime ministers of Britain and Ireland were naturally basic participants, as was Marjorie (Mo) Mowlam, Britain's Secretary of State for Northern Ireland. George Mitchell, who chaired the discussions, played a leading role, and President Clinton made a significant contribution. Other were the presidents of the European Commission, Jacques Delors of France until 1995, then Jacques Santer of Luxembourg, former Prime Minister Harri Holkerri of Finland, who represented the United Nations, and General John de Chastelain of Canada who took on the difficult job of monitoring the decommissioning of weapon by the paramilitaries.
13. Louis MacNeice (1907–1963) who was born in Belfast has been considered the major Irish poet after Yeats.
14. "We shall overcome" were not the words of King, but the song of the civil rights movement, which he would have sung with the crowds at almost every public meeting.
15. William Wordsworth wrote in his "Lines Above Tintern Abbey that these acts were "the best portion of a good man's life."
16. Edmund Burke (1729–1797) was a parliamentarian, a famous orator and political writer.
17. Amos Oz (1939–). Major Israeli author who has worked prominently for a just peace with the Palestinians. He has won international awards both for literature and for peace.
    George F. Kennan (1904–2005), American diplomat and historian. His famous

"long telegram" about containment of the Soviet Union sent from the Moscow Embassy in 1946 became the American policy in the Cold War, but with an emphasis upon military means rather than the diplomatic and economic measures he had recommended.
18. Plato was a Greek philosopher who wrote the *Republic* probably during the 4th century B.C. Trimble is concerned about how his ideas about "abstract perfection" have had an unfortunate influence upon Jean Jacques Rousseau, the 18th century French political philosopher and writer, as well upon modern social movements desiring to change society by revolutionary violence.
19. The Jacobins were the extremist party in the French Revolution who preferred the method of the guillotine.
20. Eoghan Harris is a political journalist in Northern Ireland.
21. Trimble urges the Palestinian Liberation Organization to deal with the fanatics of the organization Hammas, who have approved using violence against the Israeli occupation authorities.
22. The devastating bombing at Omagh in Northern Ireland in 1998 was committed by dissident members of the IRA who called themselves the Real IRA.
23. John Bunyan, a 17th century preacher was the author of the religious allegory, *The Pilgrim's Progress*, which still has many readers today.
24. Samuel Beckett (1906–1989) was an Irish novelist and playwright.
25. Sir Lewis B. Namier (1888–1960) was a British historian.
26. Bosnia and Kosovo were territories involved in the wars in former Yugoslavia. In Africa there was conflict in the state of Somalia and genocide in Rwanda.

SELECTED BIBLIOGRAPHY

By John Hume

Comments at Centennial Symposium, Oslo, 2001, http://nobelprize.org/peace/laureates/1998/hume-symp.html. *A New Ireland: Politics, Peace and Reconciliation.* Boulder, Colorado: Roberts Rinehart, 1996.

By David Trimble

Comments at Centennial Symposium, Oslo, 2001, http://nobelprize.org/peace/laureates/1998/trimble-symp.html. *North Ireland: Essays and Articles 1998–2001.* Belfast: Belfast Press, 2001.

"The United Nations Left Us No Option but to Act," in *The Iraq War and Its Consequences*, eds. Irwin Abrams and Wang Gungwu (Singapore: World Scientific, 2003): 11–15.

Other Sources

Adams, Gerry, *A Farther Shore. Ireland's Long Road to Peace.* New York: Random House, 2003. How the longtime leader of Sinn Fein sees it.

Beggan, Dominic and Rathnam Indurthy, "Explaining Why the Good Friday Accord Is Likely to Bring a Lasting Peace in Northern Ireland," *Peace & Change*, 27 (July 2002): 331–356. Good on peace process leading to establishment of power-sharing government in December 1999, although overly optimistic about following developments. Includes 1999 interview with Gerry Adams.

Cox, Michael, Adrian Guelke and Iona Stephen, eds. *A Farewell to Arms? From "Long War" to Long Peace in Northern Ireland.* Manchester and New York: Manchester University Press, 2000.

"David Trimble," *Current Biography*, 2000. Useful for background, but misses role of Hume in Good Friday Agreement.

Drower, George. *John Hume, Peacemaker.* London: Gollancz, 1995.

Elliott, Sidney and Wm. D. Flackes. *Northern Ireland: A Political Directory, 1968–1999.* Belfast: Blackstaff Press, 1999.

Ellison, Graham. *The Crowned Harp: Policing Northern Ireland.* London: Plato, 2000.

English, Richard. *Armed Struggle: The History of the IRA.* Oxford: Oxford University Press, 2003. By professor of politics at Queen's University, Belfast, who has written widely on Northern Ireland. This book has won several awards and is highly recommended.

Farren, Sean. *Paths to a Settlement in Northern Ireland.* Gerrards Cross: Colin Smythe, 2000.

Godson, Dean. *Himself Alone: David Trimble and the Ordeal of Unionism.* London: Harper Collins, 2004.

Hennessey, Thomas. *The Northern Ireland Peace Process: Ending the Troubles?* New York: Palgrave, 2001. The peace movement in the 20th century, with special attention to politics and government since 1969.

Higgins, Tanya and Nancy Brown Diggs. *A Look at Life in Northern Ireland: How do Women Live in Culture Driven by Conflict?* Lewiston, N.Y.: Edwin Mellen Press, 2000.

Holland, Jack. *Hope against History. The Course of Conflict in Northern Ireland.* New York: Holt, 1999. Recommended.

Kaput, Raman and Jim Campbell. *The Troubled Mind of Northern Ireland: Analysis of the Emotional Effects of the Troubles.* London: Kaznac, 2004. Includes psychoanalytical perspective.

Maguire, Mairead Corrigan. *The Vision of Peace. Faith and Hope in Northern Ireland.* John Dear, ed., New York: Orbis, 1999. A voice for nonviolence by the 1976 Nobel laureate.

McDonald, Henry, *Trimble.* London: Bloomsbury, 2000.

McGary, John. *Northern Ireland and the Divided World: The Northern Ireland Conflict and the Good Friday Agreement in Comparative/Perspective.* Oxford and New York: Oxford University Press, 2001.

McGary, John, and Brendan O'Leary. *The Northern Ireland Conflict: Consociational Engagements.* Oxford and New York: Oxford University Press, 2004.

Mitchell, George J., *Making Peace,* New York: Knopf, 1999. A personal account of his peace mission to Northern Ireland.

Morrissey, Mike. *Northern Ireland after the Good Friday Agreement: Victims, Grievance and Blame.* London, 2002.

Mulholland, Marc. *Northern Ireland's Troubled History.* Oxford: Oxford University Press, 2002.

Murray, Gerard. *John Hume and the SDLP: Impact and Survival in Northern Ireland.* Dublin: Irish Academic Press, 1998.

Porter, Norman. *The Elusive Quest: Reconciliation in Northern Ireland.* Belfast: Blackstaff, 2003.

Rose, Peter. *How the Troubles Came to Northern Ireland.* Basingstoke: Palgrave, 2001.

Routledge, Paul, *John Hume.* London: Harper Collins, 1997. Well-illustrated. Sympathetic.

Ruane, Joseph and Jennifer Todd, eds. *After the Good Friday Agreement: Analysing Political Change in Northern Ireland.* Dublin: University College Dublin Press, 1999.

Peace 1999

MÉDECINS SANS FRONTIÈRES

in recognition of the organization's pioneering humanitarian work on several continents

INTRODUCTION

The organization Doctors Without Borders (Médicins Sans Frontières or MSF) was recognized "in recognition of its pioneering humanitarian work." Chairman Sejersted of the Norwegian Nobel Committee explains in his speech of presentation that MSF were not only doing humanitarian work in their medical relief, as earlier humanitarian prizewinners had done, such as the Red Cross, whose founder had shared the very first prize of 1901, but the MSF workers were blazing "new trails in international humanitarian work." They reached those in need quickly, they demanded freedom to decide for themselves whom to help according to purely humanitarian criteria; and they insisted on making known any violations of human rights.

Chairman Sejersted tells how critics of this first prize complained that it did nothing for peace, but only "humanized" war. Actually, he points out, it implemented Nobel's phrase in his will that the prize should go to those working not only for disarmament and the holding of peace congresses, but also for those working for "fraternity among nations." This clearly includes humanitarian efforts, and Chairman Sejersted declares, "The decision to award the first Peace Prize to humanitarian work was one of the most important decisions in the history of the prize." Later Norwegian Nobel Committees broadened the interpretation of that phrase to mean "brotherhood among peoples." And they gave the prize for other humanitarian efforts, such as work for refugees, efforts for war relief and reconstruction and for UNICEF.

Chairman Sejersted says that a second major decision of the Norwegian Nobel Committees was to decide that a true peace must be based upon the recognition of human rights and that violation of human rights also means a threat to peace. He refers to the first human rights award to Albert Lutuli in 1960 for his opposition to apartheid in South Africa and lists some of the later human rights awards. He then discusses the problems of humanitarian interventions which the Doctors Without Borders have encountered.

President James Orbinski of MSF opens his Nobel Lecture with an appeal to the government of Russia to stop "the bombing of defenseless civilians in Chechnya," declaring, "If conflicts and wars are an affair of state, violations of humanitarian law, war crimes and crimes against humanity apply to all of us." "Ours is the ethic of refusal," he says. For MSF, the humanitarian act is to seek to relieve suffering, to seek to restore autonomy, to witness to the truth of injustice, and to insist on political responsibility. Most of his lecture is devoted to this conceptp of humanitarian relief, giving examples of how humanitarianism must be kept separate from politics and from military action.

At the end of his presentation speech, Sejersted strikes an optimistic note. He is happy just before the century's end to point out that the final Peace Prize brings together two major critieria for the decisions of the Norwegian Nobel Committees, humanitarianism and human rights.

ANNOUNCEMENT

The Norwegian Nobel Committee has decided to award the Nobel Peace Prize for 1999 to Doctors Without Borders (Médecins Sans Frontières), in recognition of the organization's pioneering humanitarian work on several continents.

Since its foundation in the early 1970s, Doctors Without Borders has adhered to the fundamental principle that all disaster victims, whether the disaster is natural or human in origin, have a right to professional assistance, given as quickly and efficiently as possible. National boundaries and political circumstances or sympathies must have no influence on who is to receive humanitarian help. By maintaining a high degree of independence, the organization has succeeded in living up to these ideas.

By intervening so rapidly, Doctors Without Borders calls public attention to humanitarian catastrophes, and by pointing to the causes of such catastrophes, the organization helps to form bodies of public opinion opposed to violations and abuses of power.

In critical situations, marked by violence and brutality, the humanitarian work of Doctors Without Borders enables the organization to create openings for contacts between the opposed parties. At the same time, each fearless and self-sacrificing helper shows each victim a human face, stands for respect for that person's dignity, and is a source of hope for peace and reconciliation.

PRESENTATION

Speech by Professor Francis Sejersted, Chairman of the Norwegian Nobel Committee, on the occasion of the award of the Nobel Peace Prize for 1999, Oslo, December 10, 1999.

Translation of the Norwegian text.

Your Majesties, Your Royal Highness, Excellencies, Ladies and Gentlemen,

Few aims can be more praiseworthy than to combat suffering: to help those in the most desperate situations, whatever their race and wherever they may be, to return to a dignified life. Some persons even have the necessary strength and drive to live up to this ideal. We welcome a few of them today. We do so humbly, recognising that they are representatives of a much greater number of self-sacrificing men and women all over the world. Our thoughts go not least to those who, at this very moment, are working under the most difficult conditions, often putting their own lives at risk, in scenes of the profoundest suffering and degradation.

Every year, Médecins Sans Frontières send out over 2,500 doctors, nurses and other professional helpers to more than 80 countries, where they co-operate with a good 15,000 local personnel. They go where need, suffering and hopelessness are greatest, indeed often catastrophic in nature, regardless of whether the catastrophes are human or natural in origin. We find them in the world's countless refugee camps, as well as among Chinese peasants, Russian prisoners, or the western world's modern city slum-dwellers. They are present in large numbers in Africa — the forgotten continent.

The modest beginnings of Médecins Sans Frontières go back to the early 1970s, and a small group of French doctors formed under the leadership of Bernard Kouchner. What triggered them was their experience of emergency aid work in two disasters, one natural — the great flood in East Pakistan (later Bangladesh) — and one man-made — the cruel conflict in Biafra from 1967 to 1970.[1] Some of the doctors who provided emergency aid in those disaster areas were frustrated at finding their work impeded by complicated procedures and principles of neutrality. The new organization would have to be un-bureaucratic, flexible, and willing to take risks.

Médecins Sans Frontières blazed new trails in international humanitarian work. The organization reserved the right to intervene to help people in need irrespective of prior political approval. The essential points for Médecins Sans Frontières are to reach those in need of help as quickly as possible, and to maintain impartiality. They demand freedom to carry out their medical mandate, and to decide for themselves whom to help according to purely humanitarian criteria. What is more, they insist on making human rights violations known. In addition to helping, in other words, they also seek to draw attention to the *causes* of humanitarian catastrophes. To alleviate distress one must also get to its roots. These were new principles in the field of aid, and have not been uncontroversial. Some said that this was to confuse the issues in ways which might block access to suffering people. Médecins Sans Frontières have been called emergency aid rebels.

The first Nobel Prizes were awarded in 1901, nearly a hundred years ago, at the beginning of the century which will draw to a close in less than a month's time. The first Peace Prize went to Henri Dunant, founder of the Red Cross, who shared it with the peace activist Frédéric Passy. Dunant was goaded into action by happening to be an eye-witness to the incredible carnage at the battle of Solferino in northern Italy in 1859. The award to Dunant came in for criticism. Humanitarian work was not relevant to peace, ran the argument, but simply "humanised" war. There were, however, grounds for the decision in Nobel's will, which mentions "fraternity between nations" as one of the criteria for the Peace Prize. What better or more direct expression can there be of this idea of fraternity than to hold out a helping hand to a sufferer, regardless of identity or party?

The peace Alfred Nobel was thinking of when he established the prize was a peace that is rooted in men's hearts and minds. By showing each victim a human face, by showing respect for his or her human dignity, the fearless and selfless aid worker creates hope for peace and reconciliation. That brings us to the heart of the matter, to absolutely fundamental prerequisites for peace. The decision to award the first Peace Prize to humanitarian work was one of the most important decisions in the history of the prize. That we are continuing, at the end of the century, and the millennium, to recognise humanitarian work confirms that the course plotted then was the right one.

But in the meantime, the world has changed. We are constantly having to face new challenges. The historian Eric Hobsbawm[2] has labelled the century which is now ending "The Age of Extremes." What he has in mind is this century's totalitarian regimes. We have witnessed man-made catastrophes that spread far beyond the battlefields, systematic violations of human rights, ethnic cleansing and genocide. We have been forced to acknowledge the close connection between war or the threat of war and those systematic breaches of human rights. The threat to peace, to real peace, was more extensive than the peace campaigners had imagined at the beginning of the century.

This way of thinking began making itself felt in international work after the second world war, but only slowly. Measures against violations of human rights necessarily present challenges to the established principle of non-intervention. This principle has for a long time been regarded as fundamental to peace work, and, is still current, although today it is being confronted ever more strongly by demands for intervention against breaches of human rights. The Norwegian Nobel Committee made its first purely human rights award in 1960, to Albert Lutuli of South Africa. Since then this has been a major criterion for Peace Prize awards, as can be seen from the awards to Martin Luther King, Andrei Sakharov, Lech Walesa, Aung San Suu Kyi, and Carlos Belo, among many others. Those awards, too, were criticised for not being relevant to peace. Many of them gave rise to disputes and protests, principally from the laureates' home countries, as amounting to intervention in internal affairs.

A characteristic feature of Médecins Sans Frontières is that, more clearly than anyone else, they combine in their work the two criteria we have mentioned, humanitarian work and work for human rights. They achieve this by insisting on their right to arouse public opinion and to point to the causes of the man-made catastrophes, namely systematic breaches of the most fundamental rights. The award to Médecins Sans Frontières is first and foremost a humanitarian award, maintaining the tradition that goes back to the first award, but it is also a human rights award, and as such it links up with more recent developments in the history of the Peace Prize.

Like the Nobel Committee's human rights awards, the exposures by Médecins Sans Frontières of violations of human rights began during the cold war, when they were chiefly aimed at the brutality of communist regimes. Since the end of the cold war, the need for humanitarian intervention has certainly not diminished; meanwhile, however, the situations have grown more complex, more chaotic. "War" has turned into something other, and much less clearly definable, than a struggle between the armed forces of identifiable nations. Military units have been dissolved into armed bands. It is often difficult to name those responsible, or to find anyone to negotiate with. And the victims of these wars are not first and foremost the soldiers, as at Solferino, but the civilian populations, the women and the children.

The changed nature of war requires reassessments of strategies for peace. Humanitarian interventions, with or without peace-keeping or other forces, are figuring ever more prominently in such strategies today. Humanitarian interventions have also become important features of the foreign policies of many states. In this connection, voluntary organizations (NGOs) are finding ever more important parts to play. But the politicization of aid work, with voluntary organizations integrating ever more closely with governments, is creating new problems. Situations may easily arise in which motives are unclear and the allocation of functions can be questioned.

On the other hand, we hear talk of "the humanitarian trap." How can you help the victims without at the same time helping their executioners? There have been cases of military groups imposing starvation on a region and then stealing the aid when it arrives. There are brutal regimes which deliberately exploit the aid organizations. Knowledge that someone will care for them swells the flood of refugees — which can contribute to ethnic cleansing. For these reasons, Médecins Sans Frontières have on one or two occasions withdrawn from involvement. The genocide in Rwanda in 1994 led to a huge influx of refugees into the neighbouring state of Zaire. Médecins Sans Frontières were on the spot throughout, but for a time the organization withdrew from the refugee camps in Zaire, in protest against the abuse of aid and the terrorising of refugees by extremists. Médecins Sans Frontières followed their protest up with an appeal to world opinion. That was also the first occasion on which the organization called for military intervention to put a stop to brutality.

Médecins Sans Frontières are generally highly critical of humanitarian intervention by military force. They believe experience has shown them how a humanitarian/military alliance can introduce the logic of war and break down the humanitarian aspect of a mission. In some cases it also increases the risk to the humanitarian aid workers themselves, as happened in Iraq, Somalia and Bosnia. Médecins Sans Frontières do not want military protection, and all their vehicles are clearly marked with a symbol showing that they are unarmed: a submachine-gun with a heavy cross painted over it.

Henri Dunant imagined that there was a neutral zone, which lay outside the spheres of interest of the warring parties and which one could therefore enter with humanitarian aid. Today we see such "humanitarian zones" invaded by both sides, obliging aid organizations to make political choices and take positions on complicated moral issues. It is precisely in such situations that it becomes especially necessary to preserve one's independence. Médecins Sans Frontières are among the organizations which attach the greatest importance to independence, insisting among other things that half their revenues must come from private donors.

A large number of aid organizations are extensively and selflessly engaged in alleviating suffering all over the world. They all deserve our gratitude and our attention. Médecins Sans Frontières have a distinctive profile, and have managed to preserve many of their original virtues. They are frequently the first to arrive at the scene of a disaster. The organization remains pervaded by idealism and willingness to take great risks. It has kept its independence, and seeks systematically to draw attention to violations and distress.

Equally important is the fact that Médecins Sans Frontières have indicated, more clearly than any other organization, how burdened aid work is in our chaotic world with political and moral dilemmas. The organization has tried in various ways to adapt to this, and has, sometimes through provocative initiatives, set in motion an absolutely essential discussion of the problematic nature of humanitarian interventions, not only in their aims but also and chiefly in their consequences. Good deeds are important, but they should also lead to good results. Here as so often in life, a balance has to be found between an ethics of conviction and an ethics of responsibility. Through their strategy and their initiatives, Médecins Sans Frontières have unquestionably influenced the whole development of international aid work.

Let us in conclusion remind ourselves that, however chaotic a situation may be, or however difficult the choices one faces, one consideration remains paramount. That is to reduce distress and alleviate suffering. Médecins Sans Frontières provide professional assistance — efficiently — to people who are suffering or in need. The organization stands for an open helping hand, extended across borders, through conflicts, and into political chaos. It is by never compromising over this paramount mandate that one can achieve outward legitimacy and inner inspiration. This self-sacrificing commitment kindles in us all the belief that the next century may be better and more peaceful than this century's age of extremism. It is this self-sacrificing effort which we honour here today.

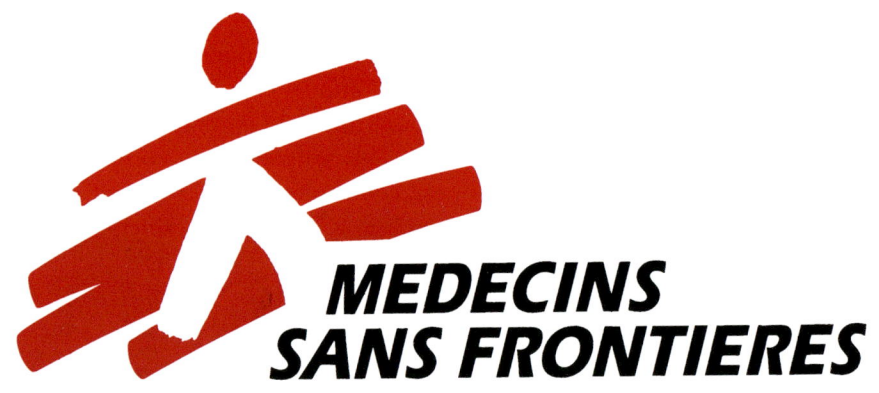

MÉDECINS SANS FRONTIÈRES (MSF)*
DOCTORS WITHOUT BORDERS

Médecins Sans Frontières (MSF) is an international humanitarian aid organisation that provides emergency medical assistance to populations in danger in nearly 70 countries. In countries where health structures are insufficient or even non-existant, MSF collaborates with authorities such as the Ministry of Health to provide assistance. MSF works in rehabilitation of hospitals and dispensaries, vaccination programmes and water and sanitation projects. MSF also works in remote health care centres, slum areas and provides training of local personnel. All this is done with the objective of rebuilding health structures to acceptable levels.

Raising Awareness

In carrying out humanitarian assistance, MSF seeks also to raise awareness of crisis situations; MSF acts as a witness and will speak out, either in private or in public about the plight of populations in danger for whom MSF works. In doing so, MSF sets out to alleviate human suffering, to protect life and health and to restore and ensure respect for the human beings and their fundamental human rights.

Only a small percentage of the populations that find themselves in a situation of danger gain the attention of the media. MSF teams travel to places that many people have never heard of, to assist those who have fallen victim to natural or man-made disasters. MSF volunteers have a story to tell when they return from their missions, and they use their experiences to speak of what they have seen. For MSF, raising awareness for these populations and the situations they are in is an important task. Whenever possible, MSF volunteers give interviews and make presentations. MSF offices worldwide facilitate the organisation of gatherings, for individuals and groups who want to speak in their home communities. MSF also mounts exhibitions and, from time to time, releases publications, with the aim of raising awareness.

It is part of MSF's work to address any violations of basic human rights encountered by field teams, violations perpetrated or sustained by political

---

*This basic description of Doctors Without Borders is presented on its website under the rubric: "About MSF." It is used here with the consent of the organization. The link is <http://www.msf.org/msfinternational/aboutmsf?>

actors. It does so by confronting the responsible actors themselves, by putting pressure on them through mobilisation of the international community and by issuing information publicly. In order to prevent compromise or manipulation of MSF's relief activities, MSF maintains neutrality and independance from individual governments. The organisation also tries to ensure that the majority of funds raised for its work comes directly from contributions from the general public. In this way, MSF guarantees equal access to its humanitarian assistance.

MSF has been setting up emergency medical aid missions around the world since 1971.

NOBEL LECTURE

December 10, 1999

by

James Orbinski

Your Majesties, Your Royal Highness, Members of the Norwegian Nobel Committee, Excellencies, Ladies and Gentlemen,

The people of Chechnya — and the people of Grozny — today and for more than three months, are enduring indiscriminate bombing by the Russian army.[3] For them humanitarian assistance is virtually unknown. It is the sick, the old and the infirm who cannot escape Grozny. While the dignity of people in crisis is so central to the honor you give today, what you acknowledge in us is our particular response to it. I appeal here today to his excellency the Ambassador of Russia and through him, to President Yeltsin, to stop the bombing of defenseless civilians in Chechnya. If conflicts and wars are an affair of the state, violations of humanitarian law, war crimes and crimes against humanity apply to all of us.

Let me say immediately that the extraordinary distinction that the Nobel Committee has given Médecins Sans Frontières is one that we accept with sincere gratitude, but also a profound discomfort in knowing that the dignity of the excluded is assaulted daily. These are the forgotten populations in danger, like the street children who struggle each grinding hour to live off the waste of those who are "included" in the social and economic order. These too are the illegal refugees that we work with in Europe, denied political status, and afraid to seek health care, lest this contact leads to their expulsion.

Our action is to help people in situations of crisis. And ours is not a contented action. Bringing medical aid to people in distress is an attempt to defend them against what is aggressive to them as human beings. Humanitarian action is more than simple generosity, simple charity. It aims to build spaces of normalcy in the midst of what is abnormal. More than offering material assistance, we aim to enable individuals to regain their rights and dignity as human beings. As an independent volunteer association, we are committed to bringing direct medical aid to people in need. But we act not in a vacuum, and we speak not into the wind, but with a clear intent to assist, to provoke change, or to reveal injustice. Our action and our voice is an act of indignation, a refusal to accept an active or passive assault on the other.

The honor you give us today could so easily go to so many organizations, or worthy individuals, who struggle in their own society. But clearly, you have made a choice to recognize MSF. We began formally in 1971 as a group of French doctors and journalists who decided to make themselves available to assist. This meant sometimes a rejection of the practices of states that directly assault the dignity of people. Silence has long been confused with neutrality, and has been presented as a necessary condition for humanitarian action. From its beginning, MSF was created in opposition to this assumption. We are not sure that words can always save lives, but we know that silence can certainly kill. Over our 28 years we have been — and are today — firmly and irrevocably committed to this ethic of refusal. This is the proud genesis of our identity, and today we struggle as an imperfect movement, but strong in thousands of volunteers and national staff, and with millions of donors who support both financially and morally, the project that is MSF. This honor is shared with all who in one way or another, have struggled and do struggle every day to make live the fragile reality that is MSF.

Humanitarianism occurs where the political has failed or is in crisis. We act not to assume political responsibility, but firstly to relieve the inhuman suffering of failure. The act must be free of political influence, and the political must recognize its responsibility to ensure that the humanitarian can exist. Humanitarian action requires a framework in which to act.

In conflict, this framework is international humanitarian law. It establishes rights for victims and humanitarian organisations and fixes the responsibility of states to ensure respect of these rights and to sanction their violation as war crimes. Today this framework is clearly dysfuntional. Access to victims of conflict is often refused. Humanitarian assistance is even used as a tool of war by belligerents. And more seriously, we are seeing the militarisation of humanitarian action by the international community.

In this dysfunction, we will speak out to push the political to assume its inescapable responsibility. Humanitarianism is not a tool to end war or to create peace. It is a citizens' response to political failure. It is an immediate, short term act that cannot erase the long term necessity of political responsibility.

And ours is an ethic of refusal. It will not allow any moral political failure or injustice to be sanitized or cleansed of its meaning. The 1992 crimes against humanity in Bosnia-Herzegovina. The 1994 genocide in Rwanda. The 1997 massacres in Zaire. The 1999 actual attacks on civilians in Chechnya. These cannot be masked by terms like "Complex Humanitarian Emergency," or "Internal Security Crisis." Or by any other such euphemism — as though they are some random, politically undetermined event. Language is determinant. It frames the problem and defines response, rights and therefore responsibilities. It defines whether a medical or humanitarian response is adequate. And it defines whether a political response is inadequate. No one calls a rape a complex gynecologic emergency. A rape is a rape, just as a genocide is a genocide. And both are a crime. For MSF, this is the humanitarian act: to seek to relieve suffering, to seek to restore autonomy, to witness to the truth of injustice, and to insist on political responsibility.

The work that MSF chooses does not occur in a vacuum, but in a social order that both includes and excludes, that both affirms and denies, and that both protects and attacks. Our daily work is a struggle, and it is intensely medical, and it is intensely personal. MSF is not a formal institution, and with any luck at all, it never will be. It is a civil society organization, and today civil society has a new global role, a new informal legitimacy that is rooted in its action and in its support from public opinion. It is also rooted in the maturity of its intent, in for example the human rights, the environmental and the humanitarian movements, and of course, the movement for equitable trade. Conflict and violence are not the only subjects of concern. We, as members of civil society, will maintain our role and our power if we remain lucid in our intent and independence.

As civil society we exist relative to the state, to its institutions and its power. We also exist relative to other non-state actors such as the private sector. Ours is not to displace the responsibility of the state. Ours is not to allow a humanitarian alibi to mask the state responsibility to ensure justice and security. And ours is not to be co-managers of misery with the state. If civil society identifies a problem, it is not theirs to provide a solution, but it is theirs to expect that states will translate this into concrete and just solutions. Only the state has the legitimacy and power to do this. Today, a growing injustice confronts us. More than 90% of all death and suffering from infectious diseases occurs in the developing world. Some of the reasons that people die from diseases like AIDS, TB, Sleeping Sickness and other tropical diseases is that life saving essential medicines are either too expensive, are not available because they are not seen as financially viable, or because there is virtually no new research and development for priority tropical diseases. This market failure is our next challenge. The challenge however, is not ours alone. It is also for governments, International Government Institutions, the Pharmaceutical Industry and other NGOs to confront this injustice. What we as a civil society movement demand is change, not charity.

We affirm the independence of the humanitarian from the political, but this is not to polarize the "good" NGO against "bad" governments, or the "virtue" of civil society against the "vice" of political power. Such a polemic is false and dangerous. As with slavery and welfare rights, history has shown that humanitarian preoccupations born in civil society have gained influence until they reach the political agenda. But these convergences should not mask the distinctions that exist between the political and the humanitarian.

Humanitarian action takes place in the short term, for limited groups and for limited objectives. This is at the same time both its strength and its limitation. The political can only be conceived in the long term, which itself is the movement of societies. Humanitarian action is by definition universal, or it is not. Humanitarian responsibility has no frontiers. Wherever in the world there is manifest distress, the humanitarian by vocation, must respond. By contrast, the political knows borders, and where crisis occurs, political response will vary because historical relations, balance of power, and the interests of one or the other must be considered. The time and space of the humanitarian are not those of the political. These vary in opposing ways, and this is another way to locate the founding principles of humanitarian action: the refusal of all forms of problem solving through sacrifice of the weak and vulnerable. No victim can be intentionally discriminated against, OR neglected to the advantage of another. One life today cannot be measured by its value tomorrow: and the relief of suffering "here," cannot legitimize the abandoning of relief "over there." The limitation of means naturally must mean the making of choice, but the context and the constraints of action do not alter the fundamentals of this humanitarian vision. It is a vision that by definition, must ignore political choices.

Today there is a confusion and inherent ambiguity in the development of socalled "military humanitarian operations." We must reaffirm with vigor and clarity the principle of an independent civilian humanitarianism. And we must criticize those interventions called "military-humanitarian." Humanitarian action exists only to preserve life, not to eliminate it. Our weapons are our transparency, the clarity of our intentions, as much as our medicines and our surgical instruments. Our weapons cannot be fighter jets and tanks, even if sometimes we think their use may respond to a necessity. We are not the same, we cannot be seen to be the same, and we cannot be made to be the same. Concretely, this is why we refused any funding from NATO member states for our work in Kosovo. And this is why we were critical then and are critical now of the humanitarian discourse of NATO. It is also why on the ground, we can work side by side with the presence of armed forces, but certainly not under their authority.

The debate on the *"Droit d'ingerence"* — the right of state intervention for so-called humanitarian purposes — is further evidence of this ambiguity. It seeks to put at the level of the humanitarian, the political question of the abuse of power, and to seek a humanitarian legitimacy for a security action through military means. When one mixes the humanitarian with the need for public security, then one inevitably tars the humanitarian with the security brush. It must be recalled that the UN Charter obliges states to intervene sometimes by force to stop threats to the international peace and security. There is no need, and indeed a danger, in using a humanitarian justification for this. In Helsinki this weekend governments will sit down to establish the makings of a European army, but to be available for humanitarian purposes.[4] We appeal to governments to go no further down this path of dangerous ambiguity. But we also encourage states to seek ways to enforce public security so that international humanitarian and human rights law can be respected.

Humanitarian action comes with limitations. It cannot be a substitute for political action. In Rwanda, early in the genocide, MSF spoke out to the world to demand that genocide be stopped by the use of force. And, so did the Red Cross. It was however, a cry that met with institutional paralysis; with acquiescence to self-interest, and with a denial of political responsibility to stop a crime that was "never again" to go unchallenged. The genocide was over before the UN Operation Turquoise was launched.[5]

I would like for a moment to acknowledge among our invited guests Chantal Ndagijimana . She lost 40 members of her family in Rwanda's genocide in 1994. Today she is a part of our team in Brussels. She survived the genocide, but like a million others, her mother and father, brothers and sisters did not. And nor did many hundreds of our national staff. I was Head of Mission in Kigali during that time. No words can describe the sheer courage with which they worked. No words can describe the horror that they died in. And no words can describe the deepest sorrow that I and all in MSF will carry always.

I remember what one of my patients said to me in Kigali: "Ummera, Ummera — sha." It is a Rwandan saying that loosely translated, means "courage, courage, my friend — find and let live your courage." It was said to me in Kigali at our hospital, by a woman who was not just attacked with a machete, but her entire body rationally and systematically mutilated. Her ears had been cut off. And her face had been so carefully disfigured, that a pattern was obvious in the slashes. There were hundreds of women, children and men brought to the hospital that day, so many that we had to lay them out on the street. And in many cases, we operated on them then and there, as the gutters around the hospital literally ran red with blood. She was one among many — living an inhuman and simply indescribable suffering. We could do little more for her at that moment than stop the bleeding with a few necessary sutures. We were completely overwhelmed, and she knew that there were so many others. She knew and I knew. She released me from my own inescapable hell. She said to me in the clearest voice I have ever heard "allez, allez ... ummera, ummera-sha" — "go, go ... my friend; find and let live your courage."

There are limits to humanitarianism. No doctor can stop a genocide. No humanitarian can stop ethnic cleansing, just as no humanitarian can make war. And no humanitarian can make peace. These are political responsibilities, not humanitarian imperatives. Let me say this very clearly: the humanitarian act is the most apolitical of all acts, but if its actions and its morality are taken seriously, it has the most profound of political implications. And the fight against impunity is one of these implications.

This is exactly what has been affirmed with the creation of the international criminal courts for both the Former Yugoslavia and Rwanda. It is also what has been affirmed with the adoption of statutes for an International Criminal Court.[6] These are significant steps. But today on the 51th anniversary of the Universal Declaration of Human Rights, the court does not yet exist, and the principles have only been ratified by three states in the last year. At this rate it will take 20 years before the court comes into being. Must we wait this long? Whatever the political costs of creating justice for states, MSF can and will testify that that the human costs of impunity are impossible to bear.

Only states can impose respect for humanitarian law and that effort cannot be purely symbolic. Srebrenica was apparently a safe haven in which we were present. The UN was also present. It said it would protect. It had Blue Helmets on the ground. And the UN stood silent and present — as the people of Srebrenica were massacred.[7]

After the deadly attempts of UN intervention in former Yugoslavia and Rwanda, which led to the death of thousands. MSF objects to the principles of military intervention which do not stipulate clear frameworks of responsibility and transparency. MSF does not want military forces to show that they can put up refugee tents faster than NGOs. Armies should be at the service of governments and policies which seek to protect the rights of victims.

If UN military operations are to protect civilian populations in the future, going beyond the "mea culpa" excuses of the Secretary General over Srebrenica and Rwanda, there must be a reform of peacekeeping operations in the UN. Member States of the Security Council must be held publicly accountable for the decisions that they do or do not vote for. Their right to veto should be regulated. Member States should be bound to ensure that adequate means are made available to implement the decisions they take.

Yes, humanitarian action has limits. It also has responsibility. It is not only about rules of right conduct and technical performance. It is at first an ethic framed in a morality. The moral intention of the humanitarian act must be confronted with its actual result. And it is here where any form of moral neutrality about what is good must be rejected. The result can be the use of the humanitarian in 1985 to support forced migration in Ethiopia, or the use in 1996 of the humanitarian to support a genocidal regime in the refugee camps of Goma.[8] Abstention is sometimes necessary so that the humanitarian is not used against a population in crisis. More recently, in North Korea, we were the first independent humanitarian organization to gain access in 1995. However, we chose to leave in the fall of 1998. Why? Because we came to the conclusion that our assistance could NOT be given freely and independent of political influence from the state authorities. We found that the most vulnerable were likely to remain so, as food aid is used to support a system that in the first instance creates vulnerability and starvation among millions. Our humanitarian action must be given independently, with a freedom to assess, to deliver and to monitor assistance so that the most vulnerable are assisted first. Aid must not mask the causes of suffering, and it cannot be simply an internal or foreign policy tool that creates rather than counters human suffering. If this is the case, we must confront the dilemma and consider abstention as the least of bad options. As MSF, we constantly call into question the limits and ambiguities of humanitarian action — particularly when it submits in silence to the interests of states and armed forces.

Last week, the United States Congress passed a bill authorizing direct food transfers to the Rebels in South Sudan. This is a miss-appropriation of the meaning and intent of humanitarian assistance. It makes food a fuel of war. And it is a dereliction of a state's duty to use any and all political means to address a 17-year long civil war that has left millions dead. Sudan's civil war today is a human misery where millions are displaced and at risk of starvation and disease; where people are bombed, robbed, looted constantly; and even enslaved, while corporate oil interests are protected, where humanitarian space is so severely restricted that it exists only in pockets; and where we and other NGOs and UN Agencies struggle to bring humanitarian assistance and protection. Is food the only political option to curb war? Food aid or humanitarian assistance, if it is to be "humanitarian assistance" — cannot be a tool in state-craft. In this case we must denounce the perfidious use of food that confuses the meaning of humanitarian assistance. If the political masks itself in an ambulance, then it is certain that the ambulance will be fired on. As well, if food is allowed to be used as a weapon of war then it also legitimates that populations can be starved as a weapon of war.

Independent humanitarianism is a daily struggle to assist and protect. In the vast majority of our projects it is played out away from the media spot-light, and away from the attention of the politically powerful. It is lived most deeply, most intimately in the daily grind of forgotten war and forgotten crisis. Numerous peoples of Africa literally agonise in a continent rich in natural resources and culture. Hundreds of thousands of our contemporaries are forced to leave their lands and their family to search for work, food, to educate their children and to stay alive. Men and women risk their lives to embark on clandestine journeys only to end up in a hellish immigration detention centre, or barely surviving on the periphery of our so called civilised world.

Our volunteers and staff live and work among people whose dignity is violated every day. These volunteers choose freely to use their liberty to make the world a more bearable place. Despite grand debates on world order, the act of humanitarianism comes down to one thing: individual human beings reaching out to their counterparts who find themselves in the most difficult circumstances. One bandage at a time, one suture at a time, one vaccination at a time. And, uniquely for Médecins Sans Frontières, working in around 80 countries, over 20 of which are in conflict, telling the world what they have seen. All this in the hope that the cycles of violence and destruction will not continue endlessly.

As we accept this extraordinary honor, we want again to thank the Nobel Committee for its affirmation of the right to humanitarian assistance around the globe. For its affirmation of the road MSF has chosen to take: to remain outspoken, passionate and deeply committed to its core principles of volunteerism, impartiality, and its belief that every person deserves both medical assistance and the recognition of his or her humanity. We would like to take this opportunity to state our deepest appreciation to the volunteers and national staff who have made these ambitious ideals a concrete reality, and who have, we believe, brought some peace to the world that has experienced such immense suffering and who are the living reality of MSF.

ENDNOTES

1. Biafra was a southeastern section of Nigeria, in which the eight million Ibo inhabitants in these years fought a bloody war to win their independence. They failed, and it is thought that one million died, mostly from starvation and illness.
2. Eric Hobsbawm is a well-known British Marxist historian. His book *The Age of Extremes* was translated into 37 languages.
3. The Russian Republic of Chechnya, with its capital city of Grozny, is located in southeastern Russia near the northwestern end of the Caspian Sea. This region has been the scene of intense battles with Russian armies as the Chechens have sought independence. The bombing of Grozny in 1999, which Orbinski criticizes, was part of the Russian effort to retake the city after the Chechens had forced Russian withdrawal in 1996. This conflict has continued unfortunately with violation of human rights by both sides.
4. On 10 December 1999, the day of Dr. Orbinski's speech, and on the following day, representatives of the eleven governments of the European Council of the European Union met in Helsinki. While measures were adopted to strengthen common security and defence policy, it was specifically stated that this process "does not imply the creation of a European army."
5. The genocide in Rwanda, which killed about one million, was ignored by the international community. Many governments even refused to call the massacres a "genocide," which would have called for intervention based on the 1948 Geneva Convention. After the genocide ended, the Hutus, who had committed the killings, feared retribution and many of them were displaced in Rwanda or refugees fleeing the country. It was then that France offered to intervene, and the UN Security Council authorized France's Operation Turquoise, which set up "Safe Humanitarian Zones" to protect displaced persons and refugees.
6. The criminal courts established for former Yugoslavia and Rwanda were both ad hoc, with time limitations. The statutes for the permanent International Criminal Court were adopted at a meeting in Rome on 17 July 1998, and the proposed treaty embodying them came into force on 1 July 2002, when the appropriate number of states had ratified it. This was the end of a long development, going back to terms of the 1948 Geneva Convention, but the court finally came into being perhaps sooner than Dr. Orbinski had anticipated.
7. In the summer of 1995 during the Bosnian War, two years after Srebrenica was declared to be a UN Safe Area, it was the scene of the worst massacre in the war. The town was a Muslim enclave in a Serb region. Besieged by Serb forces, it was protected by a small group of lightly armed UN peacekeepers from the Netherlands, to whom the inhabitants had agreed to surrender their arms. When some Dutch soldiers were taken hostage by the the Serbs, who threatened their lives if they refused, the Serbs were permitted to enter the town, where they murdered all the Muslim men and boys age 12 to 77, also hunting down those fleeing through the forest and killing a total of almost 8,000. The women and children were deported, so that the town could become Serb. While there has been some controversy about UN responsibilities, there is no question about the culpability of the Serb commanders, which the international criminal court for former Yugoslavia has made clear.
8. After the genocide in Rwanda, many refugees poured across the border to the refugee camps near Goma, a town in the eastern province of the Democratic Republic of Congo. Orbinski refers to the humanitarian help that was being given in these camps to former leaders of the genocide, who were giving misinformation to other refugees and even continuing their own killing ways.

SELECTED BIBLIOGRAPHY

By Doctors Without Borders/Médicins Sans Frontières (MSF)

See <http://www.doctorswithoutborders.org> for current information and other reports and publications, including *Newsletter MSF–USA*.

MSF. Activity Report, 1994–2003. Annual publication describing all projects. See "MSF Programs around the World." From Afghanistan to Zimbabwe.

_____. *The War Was Following Me: Ten Years of Conflict: Violence and Chaos in the Eastern Democratic Republic of Congo.* MSF, 2002.

_____. *Humanitarian Medicine — One Person at a Time* by Thomas Nierle, M.D., Direction of Operations, MSF–Switzerland. In MSF Activity Report 2002–2003. The personal experiences of an MSF doctor.

Weissman, Fabrice, ed. *In the Shadow of "Just Wars": Violence, Politics and Humanitarian Action.* Ithaca, N.Y.: Cornell University Press, 2004. Anthology of essays evaluating MSF policies and practice by MSF members, writers, journalists and others familiar with MSF field work.

Other Sources

Bortolotti, Dan. *Hope in Hell. Inside the World of Doctors Without Borders*, Richmond Hill, Ontario: Firefly Books, 2004. First complete account, based on one hundred interviews of administrators and field workers. A positive view.

Fiona, Terry. *Condemned to Repeat? The Paradox of Humanitarianism.* Ithaca, N.Y. and London: Cornell University Press, 2000. A much praised analysis by MSF Director of Research.

Jean, François. "The Problem of Medical Relief in the Chechen War Zone," in *Central Asian Survey* 152 (1996): 255–258.

Kouchner, Bernard. *Current Biography* (1993). An MSF founder, with later assignments in French government and Kosovo.

Leyton, Elliot. *Touched by Fire. Doctors Without Borders in a Third World Crisis.* Photographs by Greg Locke. Toronto: McClelland & Stewart, 1998.

Tanguy, Joelle. "Humanitarian Responsibility and Committed Action," in *Ethics and International Affairs* 13 (1999): 29–34. By an MSF executive.

Peace 2000

KIM DAE JUNG

for his work for democracy and human rights in South Korea and in East Asia in general, and for peace and reconciliation with North Korea in particular

INTRODUCTION

In 1999 the Norwegian Nobel Committee made an award to the Doctors Without Borders, which honored them both for their humanitarian relief efforts and for their defense of human rights. Now in 2000 the Committee made another double award, this time for the same person. Kim Dae-jung was honored both for his longtime work for peace and democracy as the country's leading dissident opposing an authoritarian government, and at the same time, after he had finally become president of South Korea, for his path-breaking diplomatic efforts for peace and reconciliation between South and North Korea. As in previous awards for political leaders in the Middle East and in Northern Ireland, the Committee's prize encouraged a peace process which is under way.

As Kim told in his Nobel lecture, "Five times I faced near death at the hands of dictators, six years I spent in prison, and forty years I lived under house arrest or in exile or under constant surveillance." Attempts to assassinate him failed. He explained that it was his Christian convictions as a devout Catholic which helped him to endure these experiences. He wrote from prison to one of his sons, "Only the truly magnanimous and strong are capable of forgiving and loving." These were not only just words. As president one of his first actions was to pardon a general who had condemned him to death. This was the spirit which has led him to be called "the Mandela of Asia."

Chairman Gunnar Berge of the Nobel Committee said in his presentation speech, "Kim Dae-jung's work for human rights made him a worthy candidate irrespective of the recent developments in relations between the two Korean states." He added, however, that in the past year, his reconciliation efforts "added a new and important dimension" to his candidacy for the Peace Prize.

As a dissident he had long opposed the hard-liners of the South Korean government in urging reconciliation with the North. The two Koreas remained technically at war, and for half a century strong battle lines faced one another on each side of the boundary separating them, the South Korean forces being strengthened by troops from the United States. However, early in his term as president, Kim Dae-jung followed his so-called "sunshine policy" of offering cooperation and aid to North Korea, without requiring reciprocal policy changes. Eventually, and as was later learned, with the added inducement of funds paid from the South, Kim Jong-il, dictator of the North, agreed to a summit meeting with Kim Dae-jung in June 2000. An agreement was reached for friendlier relationships, with economic terms and provisions for the continuation of humanitarian assistance by South Korea, and for cultural and other exchanges. Consequently, there were meetings of divided families, and athletes from North and South Korea marched together in the Olympic Games.

Kim Dae-jung devoted much of his lecture to this summit meeting, but he also sought to answer the critics who claimed that "western-style democracy was not suitable for Asia." Having spent many of those long prison terms in further educating himself through wide readings, he can effectively present the evidence of democratic antecedents in Asia centuries before they were seen in the West. Moreover, he could refer to the recent democratic developments in other Asian states, including the efforts of Aung San Suu Kyi in Myanmar (Burma) and the more successful establishment of a democratic independent state in East Timor, both of which he had supported. José Ramos-Horta (Peace Prize, 1996), Foreign Minister of the new East Timor Republic, was in his audience at the ceremony. Aung San Suu Kyi (Peace Prize, 1991) is working for democracy in her own country despite great opposition and has convincingly written about democracy's Asian roots. Kim Dae-Jung had domestic problems during his administration, and when he went to Washington, he was not warmly received by President Bush, who did not support Kim's "sunshine policy" toward North Korea, but who would have approved the way Kim extolled democracy in this lecture and in his writing. Whatever happens to the political evolution on the Korean peninsula, much will depend upon the future relations of the United States with North Korea, but in the history of the Nobel Peace Prize, Kim Dae-jung's lifetime of personal effort on behalf of human rights and peace will assure him a respected place.

ANNOUNCEMENT

The Norwegian Nobel Committee has decided to award the Nobel Peace Prize for 2000 to Kim Dae-jung "for his work for democracy and human rights in South Korea and in East Asia in general, and for peace and reconciliation with North Korea in particular."

In the course of South Korea's decades of authoritarian rule, despite repeated threats on his life and long periods in exile, Kim Dae-jung gradually emerged as his country's leading spokesman for democracy. His election in 1997 as the republic's president marked South Korea's definitive entry among the world's democracies. As president, Kim Dae-jung has sought to consolidate democratic government and to promote internal reconciliation within South Korea.

With great moral strength, Kim Dae-jung has stood out in East Asia as a leading defender of universal human rights against attempts to limit the relevance of those rights in Asia. His commitment in favour of democracy in Burma and against repression in East Timor has been considerable.

Through his "sunshine policy," Kim Dae-jung has attempted to overcome more than fifty years of war and hostility between North and South Korea. His visit to North Korea gave impetus to a process which has reduced tension between the two countries. There may now be hope that the cold war will also come to an end in Korea. Kim Dae-jung has worked for South Korea's reconciliation with other neighbouring countries, especially Japan.

The Norwegian Nobel Committee wishes to express its recognition of the contributions made by North Korea's and other countries' leaders to advance reconciliation and possible reunification on the Korean peninsula.

PRESENTATION

Speech by Gunnar Bérge, Chairman of the Norwegian Nobel Committee, on the occasion of the award of the Nobel Peace Prize for 2000, Oslo, December 10, 2000.

Translation of the Norwegian text.

Your Majesties, Your Royal Highnesses, Excellencies, Ladies and Gentlemen,

The Norwegian Nobel Committee has decided to award the Nobel Peace Prize for the year 2000 to Kim Dae-jung. He receives the prize for his lifelong work for democracy and human rights in South Korea and East Asia in general, and for peace and reconciliation with North Korea in particular. We welcome the Laureate here today.

The question has been raised of whether it is too early to award the prize for a process of reconciliation which has only just begun. It would suffice to say in reply that Kim Dae-jung's work for human rights made him a worthy candidate irrespective of the recent developments in relations between the two Korean states. It is also clear, however, that his strong commitment to reconciliation with North Korea, and the results that have been achieved — especially in the past year — added a new and important dimension to Kim Dae-jung's candidacy.

While recognizing that reverses in international peace work are something one has to be prepared for, the Nobel Committee nevertheless adheres to the principle: nothing ventured, nothing gained. The Peace Prize is a reward for the steps that have been taken so far. However, as so often before in the history of the Nobel Peace Prize, it is intended this year, too, as an encouragement to advance still further along the long road to peace and reconciliation.

This is to a large extent a matter of courage. Kim Dae-jung has had the will to break with fifty years of ingrained hostility, and to reach out a cooperative hand across what has probably been the world's most heavily guarded frontier. His has been the kind of personal and political courage which, regrettably, is all too often missing in other conflict-ridden regions. The same applies to peace work as to life in general when you set out to cross the highest mountains: the first steps are the hardest. But you can count on plenty of company along the glamorous finishing stretch. Gunnar Roaldkvam, a writer from Stavanger, puts this so simply and so aptly in his poem "The last drop":

Once upon a time
there were two drops of water;
one was the first,
the other the last.

The first drop
was the bravest.

I could quite fancy
being the last drop,
the one that makes everything
run over,
so that we get
our freedom back.

But who wants to be
the first
drop?

Today, Kim Dae-jung is the president of a democratic South Korea. His path to power has been long — extremely long. For decades he fought a seemingly hopeless fight against an authoritarian regime. One may well ask where he found the strength. His own answer is: "I used all my strength to resist the dictatorial regimes, because there was no other way to defend the people and promote democracy. I felt like a homeowner whose house was invaded by a robber. I had to fight the intruder with my bare hands to protect my family and property without thinking of my own safety."

In the 1950s, when Kim ran for election to the national assembly, the police were used to prevent support for any other candidates than the regime's own. He was not elected until 1961, but that success was short-lived: a military coup three days later led to the dissolution of the assembly. But Kim did not give up. In 1963, after ten years of almost continuous political struggle, he finally took a seat in the national assembly as an opposition representative. The ruling party, it should be added, tried to buy him. Kim was not for sale.

In 1971, Kim Dae-jung ran in the presidential election, winning 46 per cent of the votes despite considerable ballot-rigging. This made him a serious threat to the military regime. As a result, he spent many long years, first in prison, then in house arrest and in exile in Japan and the United States. He also underwent kidnapping and assassination attempts. Somehow enduring all these trials, Kim kept up his outspoken opposition to the regime.

As a member of a delegation from the Norwegian Storting, I visited South Korea in 1979, a visit which among other things brought me into contact with supporters of Kim Dae-jung. I am glad I was able then to serve as a link to important connections in Scandinavia.

Even under severe prison conditions, Kim Dae-jung managed to find things to live for. With indomitable optimism, he wrote about the *pleasures* he found in prison. Reading all kinds of eastern and western books: theology, politics, economics, history and literature. The brief meetings with his family. The letters from those closest to him, and the opportunities to write back, despite all the attempts to prevent him. And finally the flowers in the tiny patch of a garden where he was allowed to spend an hour a day.

Kim Dae-jung's story has a lot in common with the experience of several other Peace Prize Laureates, especially Nelson Mandela and Andrei Sakharov. And with that of Mahatma Gandhi, who did not receive the prize but would have deserved it.[1] To outsiders, Kim's invincible spirit may appear almost superhuman. On this point, too, the Laureate takes a more sober view: "Many people tell me," he says, "that I am courageous, because I have been to prison six or seven times and overcome several close calls in my life. However, the truth is that I am as timid now as I was in my boyhood. Considering what I have experienced in my life, I should not be afraid of being imprisoned. But, whenever I was locked up, I was invariably fearful and anxious." Self-knowledge of this order does not detract from the courage!

Kim Dae-jung ran in two more presidential elections, in 1987 and 1992. If no military regime stood in his way, the argument was used against him, in a country of sharp regional divisions, that he came from the wrong region. Finally wearying of the struggle, he withdrew from active politics after the 1992 election.

But in 1997 Kim Dae-jung saw a new opportunity. Incredibly enough, with his political enemies divided amongst themselves, the military regime's leading opponent was elected president. That was the definitive proof that South Korea had at long last found a place among the world's democracies.

The idea of revenge must have occurred to the new president. Instead, as with Nelson Mandela, forgiveness and reconciliation became the main planks in Kim's political platform and guided the steps he took. *Kim Dae-jung forgave most things — including the unforgivable.*

What had taken place was a democratic revolution. But even after a revolution, some features of the old order live on. In a democratic perspective, South Korea still has some way to go where reform of the legal system and of security legislation is concerned. According to Amnesty International, there are still long-term political prisoners in South Korean gaols. Others maintain that the rights of organized labour are not sufficiently safeguarded. Our reply is that we feel confident that Kim Dae-jung will complete the process of democratisation of which he has been the foremost spokesman for almost half a century.

An important debate is currently being conducted in Asia concerning the status of human rights. It is argued by some that such rights are a western invention, a tool for achieving western political and cultural dominance. Kim rejects this view, just as he also denies that there are any special Asian, as distinct from universal, human rights. The same way of thinking led the Nobel Committee, in its grounds for this year's award, to draw particular attention to the important part Kim has played in the development of human rights throughout East Asia. As José Ramos-Horta, Peace Prize Laureate in 1996 and with us here today, has stated, Kim also vigorously took up the cause of East Timor. There was great symbolic force in the decision to place the South Korean army, used only a few years previously to suppress political opposition in its own country, at the disposal of the global community in defence of human rights in East Timor.

Kim Dae-jung has also actively supported Aung San Suu Kyi, Peace Prize Laureate in 1991, in her heroic struggle against the dictatorship in Burma. Our thoughts today also reach out to her, prevented as she has so far been from coming to Norway to receive the Peace Prize she so richly deserves. Unfortunately the regime is once again stepping up its pressure on Aung San Suu Kyi.[2]

Kim was elected president on a program of extensive reforms in South Korea, and an active policy of cooperation with North Korea now widely spoken of as the "sunshine policy." The term originated in Aesop's fable about the traveller who in a strong north wind drew his cloak ever more closely about him, only to have to take it off in the end because of the warmth of the sun.

The sunshine policy is designed, if not to stop the wind, then at least to lessen the cold through gradually increasing interaction and an emphasis on the common interests of the two states. Kim Dae-jung has made it clear that South Korea has no intention of annexing or absorbing its northern neighbour. The target is reunification, although both parties know that it will take time and will require the most thorough preparation.

There can be little doubt that to date Kim Dae-jung has been the prime mover behind the ongoing process of détente and reconciliation. Perhaps his role can best be compared with Willy Brandt's, whose *Ostpolitik* was of such fundamental importance in the normalisation between the two German states, and won him the Peace Prize.[3] Brandt's *Ostpolitik* alone could not have led to German unification, but it was a prerequisite for the union which followed in 1989–90. From South Korea's point of view, the political side of Germany's unification looks attractive, while the economic side, with a price tag that may be much higher in Korea than in Germany, is a warning to make haste slowly.

The dialogue between Kim Dae-jung and Kim Jung-il at the Pyongyang summit last June led to more than loose declarations and airy rhetoric. The pictures of family members meeting after five decades of separation made a deep impression all over the world. However restricted and controlled these contacts may be, the tears of joy are a stark contrast to the cold, hatred and discouragement felt so strongly by all visitors to the border at Panmunjon.

The people of North Korea have lived under extremely difficult conditions for a long time. The international community can not be indifferent to their hunger, or remain silent in the face of the country's massive political repression. On the other hand, North Korea's leaders deserve recognition for their part in the first steps towards reconciliation between the two countries.

In most of the world, the cold war ice age is over. The world may see the sunshine policy thawing the last remnants of the cold war on the Korean peninsula. It may take time. But the process has begun, and no one has contributed more than today's Laureate, Kim Dae-jung. In the poet's words, "The first drop was the bravest."

KIM DAE-JUNG

President Kim Dae-jung was born on December 3, 1925 in a small village on an island of South Korea's southwestern coast. He graduated from a commercial high school in 1943.

When the Syngman Rhee Administration (1948–1960) began to become increasingly dictatorial, he decided to enter politics. His political career proved to be rather turbulent from the start. He was elected to the National Assembly in a bi-election in 1961 after two unsuccessful bids, but, within three days of his election, the National Assembly was dissolved following a military coup d'etat led by Major General Park Chung Hee.

When he was elected again to the National Assembly in 1963, he began to emerge as a junior leader within his own party. He served as the spokesman for the Democratic Party in 1965 and became the chairman of the party's Policy Planning Committee the following year.

As President Park Chung Hee sought constitutional revisions in 1969 to allow himself to run for a third term, Kim Dae-jung gave an address against the scheme in an outdoor rally, and he was widely acclaimed for his vision and courage. He was chosen the presidential candidate of the New Democratic Party in 1971, running against the all-powerful incumbent, Park Chung Hee. Despite the obstructionist tactics and illegal electioneering practices of the ruling party, he garnered over 46 per cent of the votes cast.

During the Assembly election campaign that soon followed the presidential vote, opposition leader Kim experienced what was to be the first of at least five attempts on his life by his political foes. A heavy-load truck rammed into his car, seriously injuring him and his two aides. President Kim still suffers from the leg injury.

Barely a year after the election. President Park imposed martial law, banned all political activities and rammed the so-called Yushin (revitalizing reform) Constitution through the National Assembly. It gave the president power for life. Kim Dae-jung strenuously objected to these extra-legal measures and led campaigns against Park's regime in the U.S. and Japan. In August 1973, agents of the Korean Central Intelligence Agency abducted Kim from a Tokyo hotel. The plot was to "eliminate" him but swift and strong reactions from the U.S. and Japan resulted in his release in Seoul a week later. He was immediately placed under house arrest.

On March 1, 1976, the indomitable opposition leader joined other democracy fighters in issuing the "Independence Day Declaration for Democratization," which touched off yet another wave of pro-democracy demonstrations in Korea. Subsequently, he was sentenced to five years in prison. He remained in jail until the authorities released him and put him under house arrest in 1978.

Soon after President Park was assassinated by one of his close aides in October 1979, Kim had his civil and political rights restored. After a few months of political unrest another group of soldiers seized power and Kim Dae-jung was thrown into prison, again, in May 1980 on charges of treason. In November of that year, a military court sentenced him to death. The sentence was later commuted to life imprisonment, and then to a 20-year term. In December 1982, his prison term was suspended, and he was allowed to travel to the United States.

Kim ended his exile in the U.S. and returned home in early 1985 despite his supporters' warnings that he might meet the same tragic fate as Philippine Senator Benigno Aquino.[4] Back in Seoul, he was immediately put under house arrest but his return intensified the nationwide pro-democracy movement. In June 1987, Kim was cleared of all outstanding charges and his civil and political rights were fully restored. He ran and was defeated in presidential elections in 1987 and 1992.

In December 1997, he was elected to the presidency, winning 40.3 per cent of the votes. When he was inaugurated as the eighth President of the Republic of Korea, it marked the first transition of power from the ruling to the opposition party in Korea's modern history.

Taking over the government in the midst of an unprecedented financial crisis, President Kim devoted himself to the task of economic recovery and managed to pull the country back from the brink of bankruptcy. Reforms and restructuring that began early in his Administration still continue.

President Kim Dae-jung's vision for the Korean people led him to pursue a policy of engagement toward North Korea. He and North Korean leader Kim Jong-il worked together on a joint declaration they signed on June 15, 2000 paving the way for a brighter future for all Koreans and other peace-loving peoples of the world.

NOBEL LECTURE

December 10, 2000

by

KIM DAE-JUNG

Your Majesty, Your Royal Highnesses, Members of the Norwegian Nobel Committee, Excellencies, Ladies and Gentlemen,

Human rights and peace have a sacred ground in Norway. The Nobel Peace Prize is a solemn message that inspires all humanity to dedicate ourselves to peace. I am infinitely grateful to be given the honor. But I think of the countless people and colleagues in Korea, who have given themselves willingly to democracy and human rights and the dream of national unification. And I must conclude that the honor should go to them.

I also think of the many countries and friends around the world, who have given generous support to the efforts of my people to achieve democratization and inter-Korean reconciliation. I thank them very sincerely.

I know that the first South-North Korean summit meeting in June and the start of inter-Korean reconciliation is one of the reasons for which I am given the Nobel Peace Prize.

Distinguished guests,

I would like to speak to you about the breakthrough in South-North Korean relations that the Nobel Committee has judged worthy of its commendation. In mid-June, I traveled to Pyongyang for the historic meeting with Chairman Kim Jong-il of the North Korean National Defense Commission. I went with a heavy heart not knowing what to expect, but convinced that I must go for the reconciliation of my people and peace on the Korean peninsula. There was no guarantee that the summit meeting would go well. Divided for half-a-century after a three-year war, South and North Korea have lived in mutual distrust and enmity across the barbed-wire fence of the demilitarized zone.

To replace dangerous stand-off with peace and cooperation, I proclaimed my sunshine policy upon becoming President in February 1998, and have consistently promoted its message of reconciliation with the North: first, we will never accept unification through communization; second, nor would we attempt to achieve unification by absorbing the North; and third, South and North Korea should seek peaceful coexistence and cooperation. Unification, I believe, can wait until such a time when both sides feel comfortable enough in becoming one again, no matter how long it takes. At first, North Korea resisted, suspecting that the sunshine policy was a deceitful plot to bring it down. But our genuine intent and consistency, together with the broad support for the sunshine policy from around the world, including its moral leaders such as Norway, convinced North Korea that it should respond in kind. Thus, the South-North summit could be held.

I had expected the talks with the North Korean leader to be extremely tough, and they were. However, starting from the shared desire to promote the safety, reconciliation and cooperation of our people, the Chairman and I were able to obtain some important agreements.

First, we agreed that unification must be achieved independently and peacefully, that unification should not be hurried along and for now the two sides should work together to expand peaceful exchanges and cooperation and build peaceful coexistence.

Second, we succeeded in bridging the unification formulas of the two sides, which had remained widely divergent. By proposing a "loose form of federation" this time, North Korea has come closer to our call for a confederation of "one people, two systems, two independent governments" as the pre-unification stage. For the first time in the half-century division, the two sides have found a point of convergence on which the process toward unification can be drawn out.

Third, the two sides concurred that the US military presence on the Korean peninsula should continue for stability on the peninsula and Northeast Asia.

During the past 50 years, North Korea had made the withdrawal of the US troops from the Korean peninsula its primary point of contention. I said to Chairman Kim: "The Korean peninsula is surrounded by the four powers of the United States, Japan, China and Russia. Given the unique geopolitical location not to be found any other time or place, the continued US military presence on the Korean peninsula is indispensable to our security and peace, not just for now but even after unification. Look at Europe. NATO had been created and American troops stationed in Europe so as to deter the Soviet Union and the East European bloc. But, now, after the fall of the communist bloc, NATO and US troops are still there in Europe, because they continue to be needed for peace and stability in Europe."

To this explanation of mine, Chairman Kim, to my surprise, had a very positive response. It was bold switch from North Korea's long-standing demand, and a very significant move for peace on the Korean peninsula and Northeast Asia.

We also agreed that the humanitarian issue of the separated families should be promptly addressed. Thus, since the summit, the two sides have been taking steps to alleviate their pain. The Chairman and I also agreed to promote economic cooperation. Thus, the two sides have signed an agreement to work out four key legal instruments that would facilitate the expansion of inter-Korean economic cooperation, such as investment protection and double-taxation avoidance agreements. Meanwhile, we have continued with the humanitarian assistance to the North, with 300,000 tons of fertilizer and 500,000 tons of food. Sports, culture and arts, and tourism exchanges have also been activated in the follow-up to the summit.

Furthermore, for tension reduction and the establishment of durable peace, the defense ministers of the two sides have met, pledging never to wage another war against each other. They also agreed to the needed military cooperation in the work to relink the severed railway and road between South and North Korea.

Convinced that improved inter-Korean relations is not enough for peace to fully settle on the Korean peninsula, I have strongly encouraged Chairman Kim to build better ties with the United States and Japan as well as other western countries. After returning from Pyongyang, I urged President Clinton of the United States and Prime Minister Mori of Japan to improve relations with North Korea.

At the 3rd ASEM Leaders' Meeting in Seoul in late October,[7] I advised our friends in Europe to do the same. Indeed, many advances have recently been made between North Korea and the United States, as well as between North Korea and many countries of Europe. I am confident that these developments will have a decisive influence in the advancement of peace on the Korean peninsula.

Ladies and Gentlemen,

In the decades of my struggle for democracy, I was constantly faced with the refutation that western-style democracy was not suitable for Asia, that Asia lacked the roots. This is far from true. In Asia, long before the west, the respect for human dignity was written into systems of thought, and intellectual traditions upholding the concept of "demos" took root. "The people are heaven. The will of the people is the will of heaven. Revere the people, as you would heaven." This was the central tenet in the political thoughts of China and Korea as early as three thousand years ago. Five centuries later in India, Buddhism rose to preach the supreme importance of one's dignity and rights as a human being.

There were also ruling ideologies and institutions that placed the people first. Mencius, disciple of Confucius, said: "The king is son of heaven. Heaven sent him to serve the people with just rule. If he fails and oppresses the people, the people have the right, on behalf of heaven, to dispose of him."[5] And this, 2,000 years before John Locke expounded the theory of the social contract and civic sovereignty.[6]

In China and Korea, feudalism was brought down and replaced with counties and prefectures before the birth of Christ, and civil service exams to recruit government officials are a thousand years old. The exercise of power by the king and high officials were monitored by robust systems of auditing. In sum, Asia was rich in the intellectual and institutional traditions that would provide fertile grounds for democracy. What Asia did not have was the organizations of representative democracy. The genius of the west was to create the organizations, a remarkable accomplishment that has greatly advanced the history of humankind.

Brought into Asian countries with deep roots in the respect for demos, western democratic institutions have adapted and functioned admirably, as can be seen in the cases of Korea, Japan, the Philippines, Indonesia, Thailand, India, Bangladesh, Nepal, and Sri Lanka. In East Timor, the people went to the polling stations to vote for their independence, despite the threat to their lives from the savage militias. In Myanmar, Madam Aung San Suu Kyi is still leading the struggle for democracy. She retains wide support of the people. I have every confidence that there, too, democracy will prevail and a representative government will be restored.

Distinguished Guests,

I believe that democracy is the absolute value that makes for human dignity, as well as the only road to sustained economic development and social justice.

Without democracy the market economy cannot blossom, and without market economics, economic competitiveness and growth cannot be achieved.

A national economy lacking a democratic foundation is a castle built on sand. Therefore, as President of the Republic of Korea, I have made the parallel development of democracy and market economics, supplemented with a system of productive welfare, the basic mission of my government.

To achieve the mission, during the past two-and-a-half years, we have taken steps to actively guarantee the democratic rights of our citizens. We have also been steadfast in implementing bold reforms in the financial, corporate, public and labor sectors. Furthermore, the efforts to promote productive welfare, focusing on human resources development for all citizens, including the low-income classes, have made much headway.

The reforms will continue in Korea. We are committed to the early completion of the current reform measures, as well as to reform as an on-going process of transformation into a first-rate economy of the 21st century. This we hope to achieve by combining the strength of our traditional industries with the endless possibilities that lie in the information and bio-tech fields.

The knowledge and information age of the 21st century promises to be an age of enormous wealth. But it also presents the danger of hugely growing wealth gaps between and within countries. The problem presents itself as a serious threat to human rights and peace. In the new century, we must continue the fight against the forces that suppress democracy and resort to violence. We must also strive to deal with the new challenge to human rights and peace with steps to alleviate the information gap, to help the developing countries and the marginalized sectors of society to catch up with the new age.

Your Majesty, Your Royal Highnesses, Ladies and Gentlemen,

Allow me to say a few words on a personal note. Five times I faced near death at the hands of dictators, six years I spent in prison, and forty years I lived under house arrest or in exile and under constant surveillance. I could not have endured the hardship without the support of my people and the encouragement of fellow democrats around the world. The strength also came from deep personal beliefs.

I have lived, and continue to live, in the belief that God is always with me. I know this from experience. In August of 1973, while exiled in Japan, I was kidnapped from my hotel room in Tokyo by intelligence agents of the then military government of South Korea. The news of the incident startled the world. The agents took me to their boat at anchor along the seashore. They tied me up, blinded me, and stuffed my mouth. Just when they were about to throw me overboard, Jesus Christ appeared before me with such clarity. I clung to him and begged him to save me. At that very moment, an airplane came down from the sky to rescue me from the moment of death.

Another faith is my belief in the justice of history. In 1980, I was sentenced to death by the military regime. For six months in prison, I awaited the execution day. Often, I shuddered with fear of death. But I would find calm in the fact of history that justice ultimately prevails. I was then, and am still, an avid reader of history. And I knew that in all ages, in all places, he who lives a righteous life dedicated to his people and humanity may not be victorious, may meet a gruesome end in his lifetime, but will be triumphant and honored in history; he who wins by injustice may dominate the present day, but history will always judge him to be a shameful loser. There can be no exception.

Your Majesty, Your Royal Highnesses, Ladies and Gentlemen,

Accepting the Nobel Peace Prize, the honoree is committed to an endless duty. I humbly pledge before you that, as the great heroes of history have taught us, as Alfred Nobel would expect of us, I shall give the rest of my life to human rights and peace in my country and the world, and to the reconciliation and cooperation of my people. I ask for your encouragement and the abiding support of all who are committed to advancing democracy and peace around the world.

Thank you.

ENDNOTES

1. Nelson Mandela (1993) served 27 years in prison, and Andrei Sakharov(1975) was harassed by the Soviet government and sent to internal exile. The best explanation as to why Gandhi did not receive the Peace Prize is the article by Oyvind TØNNESSON at <http://nobelprize.org/peace/articles/gandhi/>
2. Aung San Suu Kyi is still detained by the government of Myanmar (Burma) in 2005.
3. The *Ostpolitik* (Eastern Politics) of former West German Chancellor Willy Brandt (1971) was for reconciliation with the former enemy, the Soviet Union, and to recognize the East German communist state.
4. Benigno Aquino was a leading opponent of Philippine's ex-President Marcos. When he returned from exile, he was gunned down at the airport.
5. Mencius was a Chinese philosopher who lived in the 4th and 3rd centuries B.C.
6. John Locke (1632–1704) was an English empirical philosopher who developed the theory of the social contract of the state.
7. These Asia-Europe Meetings have been held alternately in Europe and Asia since March 1996.

SELECTED BIBLIOGRAPHY

By Kim Dae-jung

Kim Dae-jung. *A New Beginning: A Collection of Essays.* Los Angeles: University of Southern California Center, 1996.

——————. *The Korean Problem.* Seoul: Kim Dae-jung Peace Foundation Press, 1994.

——————. *Mass-Participatory Economy: Korea's Road to World Economic Power.* Lanham: University Press of America, 1996. Revised and updated edition.

Speech at Nobel Peace Symposium, Oslo, December 6, 2001. Video recording: <http://nobelprize.org/peace/laureates/2000/dae-jung-symp.html>

——————. *Philosophy and Dialogues: Building Peace and Democracy.* New York: Korean Independent Monitor, 1987.

——————. *Prison Writings.* Berkeley, California: University of California Press, 1987.

Other Sources

Carpenter, Ted Galen and Doug Bandow. *The Korean Conundrum: America's Troubled Relationships with North and South Korea.* New York: Palgrave Macmillan, 2004.

Cumings, Bruce. *North Korea, Another Country.* New York: New Press, 2003. By the author of an important modern history of Korea. Many recommend his books, others object to his leftist advocacy.

Foster-Carter, Adam: "North Korea: Sunshine or Sunset?" In *World Today* 55(3)(1999):11–13.

Harrison, Selig. *Korean Endgames: A Strategy for Reunification and U.S. Disengagement.* Century Foundation Book. Princeton, N.J.: Princeton University Press, paperback edition with Afterword, 2003.

Kim, Samuel S., ed. *Korea's Democratization.* New York and Cambridge (UK): Cambridge University Press, 2003.

Martin, Bradley K. *Under the Loving Care of the Fatherly Leader: North Korea and the Kim Dynasty.* New York: Thomas Dunne, 2004.

Oberdorfer, Don. *The Two Koreas: A Contemporary History.* New York: Basic Books, revised and updated edition, 2002. Recommended.

O'Hanlon, Michael and Mike M. Mochizuki. *Crisis on the Korean Peninsula: How to Deal with a Nuclear North Korea.* New York: McGraw-Hill, 2003.

Oh, Kongdan and Ralph C. Hassig. *North Korea through the Looking Glass.* Washington, D.C.: Brookings Institution Press, 2000.